1

Contents

Daniel

"But you, Daniel, close up and seal the words

of the scroll until the time of the end.

Many will go here and there and

knowledge shall increase. – Daniel 12:4

Introduction

The premise of this book is the prophecies of Daniel, many of which have been misinterpreted in preceding years; and for the reader to gain an understanding that the fast-paced developments in the twentieth century have happened as predicted by Daniel through dreams, visions, and visitations by angels. This manuscript is written in a futurist interpretation of scriptures, as opposed to an historical or preterist view; in the sense that portions of Daniel and other prophetic books in the bible are yet to be fulfilled in a future time. Most importantly, the exegesis in this book is supported by and with scripture. Ultimately, the views of this book are an honest interpretation of scripture, but not necessarily politically correct; as it would be an injustice to all of the ancient prophets of Judea, most of which gave their lives to tell the truth, in what was transcribed into our bible. Daniel was one of those prophets, and his story is the foundation upon which much of this book is written.

Daniel was an Old Testament prophet of Israel that had been exiled to Babylon by King Nebuchadnezzar who had destroyed the temple of Solomon, the first temple in Jerusalem, in the sixth Century BC. Babylon conquered Judea and surrounding lands in 586 BC and carried the Jewish people of Jerusalem into captivity, where they would stay in exile for seventy years as foretold by the prophet Jeremiah. Daniel was a young man, and was considered worthy of special treatment by the king, as were several of his friends, to serve in the king's palace. Scriptures do not tell us much of the background of Daniel's life or family, only that he was a devout Jew that prayed regularly and humbly to God. There is no indication as to why God chose Daniel to reveal some of the most significant prophecies for our time recorded in the bible, but Daniel had an honest and open heart to God and to his fellow countrymen. We don't learn from scriptures the outcome of Daniel's life, except he was told by an angel in Daniel 12:13 *"Go your way till your end. You will rest, and then at the end of the days you will rise to receive your allotted inheritance"*. This was the last conversation in the book of Daniel; whether he died in Babylon or returned to Jerusalem is unknown, only that he is not recorded at the Jews return from captivity in other biblical books. His visions, dreams, prayers, and life under a Babylonian king have been studied and debated for more than 2500 years. The most interesting aspect of Daniel is that in each new record of a prophetic vision, he is baffled; God always had to send an angel to interpret the visions Daniel had, because he didn't understand them himself. No other prophet of Judea, except Daniel, had difficulty understanding their own prophecies; the Old Testament prophets were sought by others for answers. Daniel had no answers of his own, yet his visions are vastly descriptive of certain central, apocalyptic figures in a time we've yet to live in. In this book we expound upon Daniel's dream interpretations for King Nebuchadnezzar of a metal statue; followed by a detailed examination of his own dreams and visions of four beasts out of the sea and the conquering of Persia in a ram and a shaggy goat. We will also analyze the angelic interpretations of the little horn and the stern faced king, the seventy weeks of years, and the king of the north and king of the south. Daniel's position as a prophet to the nation of Israel was unique in that the prophecies he received were all pointing towards a future time; long after the end of his days. He never lived to see a single prophecy fulfilled, beginning with the conquering of Persia and into the twentieth century. His prophecies still resonate with urgency to modern biblical scholars when trying to understand the deeper context of his visions. The ability to discern a portion of his prophecies was lost for two millennia; students of prophecy trying to fathom the complexities of his visions before the twentieth century archived his message to historical context.

With the dawn of the twentieth century came an altogether new enlightenment; one of knowledge. With advances in every aspect of our lives, biblical scholars are able to look at certain scriptures under a different lens. A passage in Daniel could finally step forward 2500 years into the future: Daniel 12:4 *"But you, Daniel, close up and seal the words of the scroll until the time of the end. Many will go here and there and knowledge shall increase."*

Some of the prophecies of the Book of Daniel that were not clearly fulfilled in antiquity were sealed shut until the mid-twentieth century; meaning it was incomprehensible and unable to be interpreted. It would be the equivalent of someone trying to open a safe without the correct combination. The combination to the "safe" of Daniel is time; certain world events had to transpire before his visions would be understood. We are now living in the correct "combination" of time, knowledge, and the end. This book not only explores the key prophecies of Daniel, but also unlocks them.

As Christians, we are called to be "watchmen", meaning, we are to herald new prophetic insight upon receiving it to fellow brothers and sisters in Christ. In the past two decades there has been an enormous amount of hype in Hollywood about *"Armageddon"*, *" The End of the World"*, and *"Doomsday"* in cinema. Although the bible will not get any significant or accurate credit as to the origin of these films; almost every year another movie comes out from Hollywood regarding one of these topics. Even Christian fiction has received plenty of recognition in this area in "The Left Behind" series co-written by Jerry B. Jenkins and Tim Lahaye, selling more than 60 million copies in the series worldwide.

The bible is in general a negative book, it also offers hope and salvation; however, much of the bible deals with the negative consequences of mankind's actions and culminates in a final countdown to the last days before the return of Christ. This book was not written with the intention of conveying fear to the reader, but the hope of the return of Jesus Christ and his millennial reign. During this "Final Countdown", the book of Daniel goes into great detail about the actions of a certain personage Christians now commonly refer to as the "antichrist". The narrative in Daniel referring to his activities in the forty-two months preceding the return of Christ is thoroughly investigated. In Hosea 4:6-7, God states *"My people perish for lack of knowledge, because you have rejected knowledge I also reject you as my priests";* this book dispels the "lack", and seeking the knowledge of God through his word dismisses the rejection. The apostle Paul expresses, *"the gospel is veiled to those who are perishing"* (2 Corinthians 4:3). Christians are to be aware of the times we live in, as the gospel is not veiled to us. We are called *"Ambassadors of Christ"*(2 Corinthians 5:20); an ambassador is a representative of their country, and we must understand the kingdom we represent. It is clear from the perspective of Hollywood that the entire world is waiting on some cataclysmic event to occur; Christians awaiting the imminent millennial kingdom of Christ know the truth about the impending world events. I hope this book offers the reader insight into biblical prophecy that will explain the unraveling world we live in, and hope for the kingdom we know is coming.

Cradle of Civilization

"You looked, O King, and there before you stood a large statue – An enormous, dazzling statue, awesome in appearance. – Daniel 2:31

Chapter 1

✠

First Empires of the World

The first instance of Daniels' unique relationship to God as his prophet occurred in Babylon. While Daniel was in exile, King Nebuchadnezzar, king of Babylon and the most powerful ruler of the ancient world; had a dream of a large metal statue of a man. He called in his magicians and sorcerers to interpret the dream for him; however they all failed in his request. The King was told that one of the exiles could interpret the dream. Daniel prayed to the God of Israel and God revealed the dream and the meaning of the statue to him. This statue depicted the kingdoms of the world in succession beginning with Babylon, and associated each kingdom with a particular metal. The following describes the material that the statue consisted of with the corresponding kingdom below.

(DANIEL 2:31)

BABYLON – HEAD OF GOLD

MEDE/PERSIA – CHEST AND ARMS OF SILVER

GREECE – BELLY AND THIGHS OF BRONZE

ROME – LEGS OF IRON/FEET AND TOES OF IRON MIXED WITH CLAY

With the exception of Babylon, each of these kingdoms were conquered by the proceeding kingdom and ruled in its place, and all of these kingdoms ruled over Israel. Babylon was conquered by Cyrus the Persian, the Medes co-ruled with Persia. The Greeks under Alexander the Great conquered the Median Empire followed by Rome which conquered the Greeks. Each kingdom that ruled expanded its territory after successfully conquering the preceding kingdom; however, all of these kingdoms were based on the Babylonian concept of an empire. The reason for this is that the entire statue was connected to one head, Babylon; as it is with a human, the head controls the entire body. Even though Babylon was defeated in 540 BC, Babylon remained in every subsequent kingdom's political structures and spiritual influence. The political structure based on a single governor ruling over many different precincts was in use in Babylon when Daniel was exiled there. Modern society bears the mark of ancient governments. The political structure in America and many other countries is based on the governmental structure of ancient Rome which was first used in Babylon.

The remaining kingdoms that succeeded Babylon had different views of how the nation of Israel should be treated. When the Persians conquered Babylon they released the Jews from captivity and allowed them to rebuild their temple during the reign of Darius the Mede. Alexander the Great hardly gave Israel a passing glance during his military campaign, but when his kingdom was divided after his death, the subsequent Greco-Syrian rulers of the Holy Land created conflicts with Jewish religious customs. There were four kingdoms that emerged from the Greek Empire. Alexander the Great had no heirs and had died young, so his kingdom was divided into four parts and given to his four generals. Those kingdoms continued to rule until the Romans came and conquered them.

Babylon

Babylon was the wealthiest of these kingdoms; although gold is the softest metal, each kingdom decreased in wealth and luxury but increased in strength. Babylon, under King Nebuchadnezzar, is the head of the statue, and was a set prototype for the proceeding kingdoms to follow. As with a human body, the brain is located in the head and controls the rest of the body.

Upon hearing of Daniel's interpretation that his empire was the head of gold, King Nebuchadnezzar, in his pride, built a statue of himself that was six feet wide and 60 feet high made of pure gold and proclaimed that everyone was to bow down and worship it. The religious cults of Babylon worshipped many gods including the Kings of Babylon; it was this form of religious worship that angered God because Babylonian rituals included child sacrifice, shrine prostitutes and other acts that God called wickedness. Babylonian Religion is referred to as part of the ancient mystery cults that re-emerged during the Greco-Roman period. Babylon is Akkadian for "Babilani" which translates "The Gate of the Gods" and babel means confusion as when the post –diluvian (flood) people built the tower of Babel and God confused their language. The spiritual influence of Babylon still remains today, yet hidden in plain sight, and it is this form of Babylon that the Lord overthrows in Revelation.

Mede/Persian

Persia inherited the wealth of Babylon along with the other kingdoms it conquered, however, by freeing the exiles and returning their treasures, some of the wealth was transferred back to its original owners. The arms and chest of silver was a divided kingdom shared equally between the Persians and the Medes. The chest and arms are a man's upper body strength; and the chest is also where the heart is located. Cyrus the Persian saw himself as a savior to the trodden down Jewish exiles, and upon conquering the Babylonians, he released the Israelites from captivity. Under his administration history notates his human rights achievements and his humane treatment and respect of the lands and peoples he conquered. The Israelites returned to their homeland in Judea, and during the reign of Darius the Mede, the decree was put forth for the Jews to rebuild their temple.

Greece

Bronze, the belly and thighs, is a stronger metal than the other preceding kingdoms but it is also symbolic of divine judgment, as in the bronze basins, sea, bulls, and pillars in the temple that Solomon had made. Alexander the Great went on his military campaigns to avenge his father and the treatment of the Greeks by the Medes; it was at first a campaign of revenge. Many times in the Bible God lifted up a kingdom and used that kingdom to bring judgment upon another kingdom. His kingdom was divided among his four generals after his untimely death because he had no legitimate heir.

The Dynasties of those four kingdoms were:

Seleucid Empire - Mesopotamia, the southern tip of India, Iran, Iraq, Syria, and part of Turkey

Ptolemy Empire- Egypt

Lysimachus (Thrace) Empire -modern Bulgaria, some of Greece, and parts of Turkey

Cassander Empire - Macedonia and part of Greece

Two of these kingdoms were constantly at war with each other and had a dominant role historically and in the future; the Seleucid and the Ptolemy. The Seleucid Kings tried to conquer Egypt to extend their rule and Egypt would then launch a counter strike. The Seleucid dynasty was power hungry to expand their empire and they continued warring with Egypt until Rome drew a line in the sand during the rule of Antiochus Epiphanes of the Seleucid Dynasty, making him withdraw from Egypt. These four kingdoms were shown to Daniel in a vision as four horns on the head of a shaggy goat. The goat was Greece; the prominent horn was the first king, Alexander. When his horn was broken off after his death, these four horns replaced it.

Antiochus Epiphanes, a Greek tyrant who ruled the Seleucid Dynasty in 165 BC was the worst of the Seleucid rulers in his treatment of the Jews. During his reign he banned the Jews from Temple worship, abolished daily sacrifices and finally offered a pig on the altar. His actions ended after the Maccabean Revolt which lasted more than 6 years and is still celebrated at Hanukkah.

The torso is the midpoint of a body; it allows the upper body to bend, sit up, and move the upper body while the lower body remains stationary; this was Greece under Alexander's rule. The thighs are the strength in the legs allowing the body to stand, sit and move. When his kingdom was divided into four parts; only two of the four maintained their kingdom until the Romans came; this was the Seleucid and Ptolemy dynasties. The Seleucid dynasty is of importance for it depicts the linage and origin of the antichrist.

Rome

The last kingdom was Rome symbolized by two iron legs. The legs were a divided kingdom of the eastern empire of Rome and the Western Empire of Constantinople. The feet were iron mixed with clay; this was a mixture of strength and brittleness in the eastern and western empires with the merge of church and state. The strength of iron was in the Roman government as was seen in the legs, but the clay was mixed in when the Emperor Constantine legalized Christianity in 313 AD, issued in the Edict of Milan, which gave toleration to not only Christianity but all religions in the empire. In 380 AD, Christianity was declared the official religion of the Roman Empire issued by the Edict of Thessalonica; which caused all citizens to declare the faith of the bishops of Rome. The result was that traditional pagan religions of the Roman Empire were outlawed. The government of Rome did not mix with the church even though it freed Christians from 300 years of relentless persecution by the Roman government. When Rome fell in 476 AD, the Roman Catholic Church became a separate entity and continued to grow in strength and size. By the turn of the new millennium there was continuous bickering between the eastern and western churches of the empire, each feeling they were the most prominent. The outcome of this was that each side ex-communicated the other which was later referred to as the Great Schism in 1056 AD. The church in Rome was the stronger side, however, and the institution of the Vatican was formed from the western line of popes. The power that the Roman popes wielded throughout the middle Ages, without check and with no other authority over them, brought the darkest hour to the doorsteps of the only Christian church in existence. The church barely had a pulse; such atrocities as the Inquisitions, burning of heretics, and the crusades were all executed during the Middle Ages by the Church of Rome which held power over all the kings of Europe.

The ten toes are parts of that kingdom that either do not yet exist or will not have power until the time of the Antichrist (the beast from the sea in Revelation). It will be an exact mixture of the feet of ancient Rome with iron and clay. Many biblical scholars speculate on the identity of the ten toes; most believe it will be a ten nation confederation of Europe, however, the iron will be a form of government used by ancient Rome. Some components of this government structure have a modern semblance to it; such terms as executive branch, legislative branch, judiciary branch, senate, general assembly, constitution, legal rights of citizens, chief magistrates, and republic are all words of ancient Rome. Many modern nations use this form of government including America.

The clay represents religion that was incorporated as the official and only religion of that empire, so we must parallel this thought that there would be a religion that would be declared the only religion or universal religion; however, it does not necessarily indicate Roman Catholicism as *"The beast and the ten horns will hate the Roman Catholic church (the harlot)"* *(Revelation 17:16-17).*

The Romans were the last empire to rule over Israel in the ancient world. With their legs of iron, they conquered and subdued the kingdom of Greece and incorporated it into their empire. They ruled over Israel before and during the life of Christ until crucifying him and then began their anti-Christian campaigns in the Middle East. Many Christians were martyred under the rule of Rome in the early days of the church until Constantine legalized Christianity, thereby creating the Roman Catholic Church in 313 AD.

Rome found its strength when it became a united kingdom in 509 BC after overthrowing the original ruling kings of Rome and forming the first republic. Until that time Rome had been ruled by seven kings in succession:

Romulus – Began his reign in 753 BC, the city of Rome was named after this first king. He was warlike and was deified as a War God

Numa Pompilius – He had a reputation of justice and piety, he also reformed the Roman calendar

Tullus Hostilus – Extreme war-like behavior; he died a mysterious death by being burned to ashes in his home of an unknown cause

Ancus Marcius- A grandson of Numa led a peaceful reign and established industries and ports.

Lucius Tarquinius Priscus – Adopted son of Ancus, is notable for draining the swamp around the 7 hills site, founding the Roman games, Instituting the symbols for the Roman military and civil offices, and fought wars that doubled the size of Rome bringing wealth to the city.

Servius Tullius – A son-in-law of Lucius Priscus, he implemented a new constitution for Rome, and created the Roman classes and citizenship of Rome

Lucius Tarquinus Superbus - The son of Lucius Priscus and son-in-law of Servius Tullius, he is remembered negatively for use of violence and intimidation to gain control of Rome, and for murdering his father-in-law to claim the throne. He and his family were deposed and expelled from Rome after his son raped a noble woman thus ending the reign of kings in Rome.

It was during the time of these kings that Rome was established as the city of seven hills. In scriptural interpretation, "hills" and "mountains" are symbols for kingdoms. Rome is referred to many times in Revelation, but one verse in particular identifies this city;

"The seven heads are seven hills on which the woman sits. They are also seven kings. Five have fallen, one is, the other has not yet come; but when he does come, he must remain for a short while". (Revelation 17:9-10)

The formation and location of Rome by seven successive kings on seven hills are historical and geographical facts; thereby the scriptural verses referring to Rome cannot be refuted. The heads of the beast in this verse are the successive world empires of the past which the 'woman' has presided over beginning with the kingdom of Babylon and moving forward through history. Though there were seven actual kings of Rome, they were a model of the seven world empires to come.

Through this vision that Daniel interpreted for King Nebuchadnezzar, the first four kingdoms of the known world was prophetically foretold. It began in 597 BC with the Babylonian exile of the Jewish people and continued through the Fall of Rome in 476AD. Next, we will examine the successive world empires to Rome that many biblical scholars have overlooked, though they are straight from our textbooks of history.

Mystery-Babylon the Great

The Mother of Prostitutes

The woman was dressed in purple and scarlet, and was glittering with gold, precious stones and pearls. She held a golden cup in her hand, filled with abominable things and the filth of her adulteries. — Revelation 17:4-5

✝

Chapter 2

Part I

Origins of Mystery Babylon

A Basket Case

The spirit of Babylon remained after the Babylonian city was destroyed, and then began to mystically move through empires and countries. Babylon was called "wickedness", as every form of idolatry was in practice there, and her pride at realizing, in the eyes of God, she had "a head of gold" was to be her final downfall.

Mystery Babylon has its origins in a vision by the prophet Zechariah after the Jews returned from Babylonian exile. The following verses describe a conversation between an angel and the prophet Zechariah; they were discussing the contents of what was contained inside a basket with a lead lid; it was a vision of "Mystery Babylon".

Then the cover of lead was raised and there in the basket sat a woman. He said "This is wickedness" and he pushed her back into the basket and pushed the lead cover down over its mouth. (Zechariah 5:7-8)

Two female angels came and lifted up the basket and flew away with it. Zechariah wanted to know where they were going and what was to happen with the basket and the woman inside. The angel responded:

To the country of Babylonia to build a house for it. When it is ready, the basket will be set there in its place. (Zechariah 5:11)

Zechariah was a prophet of the Jewish nation when they were released from captivity *after* Babylon had been defeated by the Persians. God said Babylon would never be rebuilt after it was conquered, and more than 2500 years later, it remains uninhabited. Babylon was located in the cradle of civilization, in a lush valley along the banks of the Euphrates River; an ideal spot for a city to be rebuilt at some point during the last two and a half millennia, yet it never was. The basket with the woman inside was not being carried into what is now modern Iraq; the "Babylonia" referred to by the angel was symbolic for Rome, and the house that was to be built is the Vatican ruling the Roman Catholic Church worldwide.

There are only two kind of women referred to in the bible that does not pertain to a specific person; a woman is symbolic of a church and of the Jewish nation of Israel. The harlot of Revelation known as "Mystery Babylon" calls herself a church, yet that is not how God views her. These two symbolic 'women' are referred to by King Solomon in Proverbs Chapters seven, eight and nine. Chapter seven is a warning of the snare of the prostitute, which is symbolic for chasing after other "gods" and worldly desires; later to be 'Mystery Babylon'. Chapter eight is symbolic of (first) the nation of Israel as a light to the gentiles and being referred to as wisdom which brought forth her first born son, Jesus the Messiah; (second) as the church which is now to be the light of the world as witnesses for Christ. Christ is wisdom; therefore his church as his body is wisdom. Chapter nine compares the woman 'wisdom' to the woman 'Folly'; the woman "wisdom" serves the food as a banquet or feast where guests are invited, the woman 'Folly' invites strangers on the street in to eat with her claiming *'food eaten in secret is delicious'*. The food eaten in secret is idolatry and sin whilst assuming that God is unaware of it. "Food" as applied to both of these situations is the word of God or a false religion and sinful life.

This secret form of religion was being carried on in Israel before the Babylonian captivity, in (Ezekiel 8:9-12) God takes the prophet Ezekiel on a guided "Mystery Tour" of the temple and temple grounds. He shows him what the people of Israel were doing in "secret", which was worshiping at idol shrines, and then coming into the temple to worship God. What the Israelites didn't know, was that their idols came back with them as "crawling things" seen on the walls of the temple of God, which Ezekiel could now see as God opened his spiritual eyes. This would be a modern equivalent of someone using horoscopes or Ouija boards, and then going to church on Sunday. These things are detestable to God and are considered the same as idol worship; there are many things that are beyond the five natural senses and that happen on the spiritual plane where God operates. The first commandment given is **"Thou shall not have any other gods before me"**; being the very first commandment, it is of the most importance. Jesus confirms this when he said the most important commandment is **"Love the Lord your God with all your heart, with all your soul and with all your mind"**.

In the Old Testament God resided inside the temple; after Christ came, He resides within us; so by involving ourselves in these 'detestable' practices, we end up with these 'crawling things' on us spiritually, which are demons or demonic forces. Many Christians become involved in situations out of ignorance, believing that something mundane such as reading a daily horoscope cannot cause damage; God views it as bowing down to an idol. He is a jealous God; as a Christian we need Him in our lives daily, and should He allow a relationship with our 'idol' to continue, the ramifications would be a litany of disturbing results in our life such as nervous breakdowns, alcohol and drug dependency, and psychological problems to name a few. Too many Christians today have some of these issues and are either not forthcoming about the problematic behavior, or do not yet realize where the problems stems from. For many, believing in a spiritual plane and demonic activity are archaic and has no place in modern society except at the cinema. My question to those people would be "Did a spiritual plane and demonic activity exist in Biblical times?" There are scriptures to prove that both occurred, therefore they still exist today, whether a person believes in them or not, because God never changes. During the time of Jesus, there was much demonic activity, and the people of that time understood what demonic possession was when asking Jesus to drive the demon out of the loved one. Our society has become stupid in the name of science; it has limited itself into believing there is nothing else other than "proven science", thereby putting itself into a box. Newton, Galileo, and Copernicus would be disappointed, as they were all Christian men who viewed the world through the lens of the Creator; an Almighty God.

Part II
Babylon's Beastly Connections

Papal Rome Connections

Then the angel carried me away in the spirit into a desert. There I saw a woman sitting on a scarlet beast that was covered with blasphemous names and had seven heads and ten horns. (Revelation 17:3)

The kings of Rome had an Insignia of 12 lictors wielding fasces and bearing axes. Their attire consisted of the purple toga, red shoes and a white diadem. It is not a coincidence that these colors are still the exact colors used in the Roman Catholic Church by cardinals and bishops. This color scheme is significant biblically as it is referred to in Revelation; the Vatican is portrayed as a harlot with great wealth sitting astride a scarlet beast with seven heads. The seven heads are seven world empires as John saw them; past present and future.

The woman was dressed in purple and scarlet and was glittering with gold, precious stones and pearls. She held a golden cup in her hand, filled with abominable things and the filth of her adulteries. (Revelation 17:4)

It is not the colors themselves that are significant but what they signify; in ancient Rome, red and purple were the colors of kings and Caesars, and in the Roman Catholic Church it is still the colors of the upper hierarchy in the papal system; the colors of extreme wealth. The color purple was so rare in ancient times that it was only used by the very wealthy in society due to the cost of painstaking labor to extract the dye from 12,000 mollusks for 1.5 grams of the pure dye

I saw that the woman was drunk with the blood of the saints, the blood of those who bore testimony to Jesus. (Revelation 17:6)

Then the angel said to me, "The waters you saw where the prostitute sits are peoples, multitudes, nations and languages. (Revelation 17:15)

The prostitute is the Vatican controlling the medieval papal system, and she was seen after her "reign of terror" was completed as being drunk with the blood of the saints. Her reign of terror ended in 1798 during the French revolution. Many *'peoples and nations'* is the extent of the influence of the Catholic Church; today it is literally worldwide.

Let me take a moment to emphasize that this is not about catholic bashing; it is about prophecy and historical facts. The papal system during the medieval era and the dark ages was the most evil institution that history has ever recorded, it's only rival was the Nazi regime. This was also the only Christian Church in operation until Martin Luther began the Reformation in the fifteenth century; in essence every

31

Christian came from a catholic background when looking far enough back in history. God is also just, and the Vatican has never been repentant for its crimes against humanity; though a few of the popes have offered an apology, it was for political correctness and popularity rather than remorse. Most of the members of the current body of the Catholic Church will defend her and downplay the atrocities committed by her during that time which leaves her unrepentant. Neither has she been brought into a human court to sit on trial for crimes against humanity. The Nazi's were hunted down and brought to Nuremburg for trial but the papacy has been able to maintain its office even after it was stripped of international power. God is also holding "Her" accountable as his "supposed wife or church" yet the only thing that interested the Popes of Rome has been power over the centuries. It would be accurate to say that the pope is the most known, and almost the most influential man on earth. Biblical prophecy points to a future time when the papal system, the Vatican, and most of Rome will be decimated.

A Connection to Nineveh

Jonah was called as a prophet of God in the eighth century; in the book of Jonah, God commanded Jonah to go to the city of Nineveh and preach for forty days. Nineveh was an ancient city in Assyria that had descended into a morally bankrupt society. After Jonah preached in Nineveh, the city experienced one of the greatest revivals in recorded biblical history. Everyone in the city, from the king, to the commoner repented; Nineveh's destruction was delayed for another century, however, the city relapsed into sin and was eventually destroyed completely in 612 BC.

In Isaiah 47:1-15 there is a two-fold pronouncement of judgment that was first declared against Nineveh, calling her the "*Virgin daughter of Babylon*"; however, the entire passage has a secondary message for the Roman Catholic Church. Compare the following scriptures, the first from Isaiah describing Nineveh, the second from Nahum describing Nineveh, and the third from Revelation describing Mystery Babylon (the Roman Catholic Church):

Nineveh:

"Now then, listen you wanton creature, lounging in your security and saying to yourself 'I am, and there is none besides me. I will never be a widow or suffer the loss of children. Both of these will overtake you in a moment, on a single day: loss of children and widowhood. They will come upon you in full measure, in spite of your many sorceries and all your potent spells.'"(Isaiah 47:8-9)

Nineveh:

"of the wanton lust of a harlot, alluring, the mistress of sorceries, who enslaved nations by her prostitution and peoples by her witchcraft." (Nahum 3:4)

Mystery Babylon (The Vatican in Rome)

"In her heart she boasts, 'I sit as queen; I am not a widow, and I will never mourn'. Therefore in one day her plagues will overtake

her: death mourning and famine. She will be consumed by fire, for
mighty is the Lord God who judges her." (Revelation 18:7) By your
magic spell all the nations were led astray. In her was found the
blood of prophets and of the saints, and of all who have been
killed on the earth. (Revelation 18:23-24)

Nineveh was a daughter of a harlot, when God looked at Nineveh, he saw ancient Babylon, when God looks at the Vatican, and he sees Babylon and Nineveh; that is the "mystery or secret". They are all the same, if one ever wondered what transpired in those ancient cities to rouse God's anger, one only has to look at the history and internal workings of the Vatican in Rome.

The "bride" of Christ would never worry about being a widow, and the children are the members of the Catholic Church. The Roman Catholic Church has fooled herself for so many centuries that in this present day and age the Papacy would never assume that any of the passages are in reference to themselves.

The same charges against Mystery Babylon were brought against the ancient city of Nineveh. The entire book of Nahum describes her destruction, but it is written almost as a parallel to what will occur when the Vatican is destroyed along with a third of Rome. It is history repeating itself, as "the spirit of Babylon never died", it only went into hiding under a cloak of religion; this religion was the final house to be built for it described in the book of Zechariah. Nineveh was described as a care-free city in Nahum, and her security was her wealth accumulation, and trade with other nations; she was never going to be a widow because she wasn't married, she was a prostitute. Mystery Babylon (the Vatican) relies on its "spiritual connection" to God, along with her wealth as security, claiming that she is the bride of Christ; thereby she could never be a widow if married to God. That is the crazy concept of Mystery Babylon; it is the same as the movie "Pretty Woman" with Julia Roberts; in which the prostitute is rewarded for her lewd behavior and marries the rich husband; a debased version of *Cinderella*.

The German Connection to Rome

With her the kings of the earth committed adultery. (Revelation 17:2)

The flame of Rome never totally winked out, and many men throughout history have tried without success to revive the Roman Empire. The Popes of Europe crowned the Emperors of Germany and the name was officially changed to the Holy Roman Empire of the German Nation in 1512. The French writer Voltaire remarked *"The agglomeration which was called and still calls itself the Holy Roman Empire was neither Holy nor Roman nor an empire."* History agrees with him; under a theocratic elective monarchy, Pope Leo III crowned Charlemagne as king of the Franks in 800 AD on Christmas Day. In that one sentence the Roman Catholic Church climbed into bed with its first king and continued to do so until 1798 when her power over the kings of the earth was stripped from her by Napoleon Bonaparte during the French Revolution. Throughout the middle ages the popes wielded significant power over the affairs of men, nations, and kings. Should a king of a particular country not adhere to the requests of the Pope in power, they would be officially excommunicated from the only church in existence.

The Holy Roman Empire was not the only German connection to Rome or the last attempt at reviving the Roman Empire. The other most notorious and sinister establishment to try its hand was Adolf Hitler at the helm of the Nazi Regime in Germany. Hitler was so enamored of Rome that his insignia, the swastika (otherwise known as the Iron Cross) was a salute to Rome, as was the salute itself, with one arm raised while saying "Heil Hitler"; directly translated from the Latin phrase "Hail Caesar". The word Kaiser is derived from the word Caesar through the Holy Roman Empire. Hitler's military resembled the Roman Legions and also carried the Eagle (Aquila) standard or ensign of Rome. The irony of the entire German "would be" revival of the Roman Empire was the fact that it was the ancient nomadic tribes of Germany known as the Ostrogoths that was responsible for its fall after sacking Rome in 476 AD.

Hitler came dangerously close to the victory of a revived Roman Empire by almost conquering Europe during World War II. Had it lasted any longer; Hitler's "Final Solution" might have indeed worked. As it was, six million Jews lost their lives during the Third Reich under the administration of a man who became a head of a beast after rising to power over Germany. When reviewing history, an empire with a head of the beast is easily identified. During the course of their reign;

they brought terror, bloodshed, and tried to change the laws of the land, while trying to conquer the entire known world.

An English Connection - The Great Divorce

Henry the VIII was one of the only successful kings to break ties with the Roman Catholic Church; his empire not only remained intact, but Great Britain increased in power in the centuries following the break. Henry was seeking a divorce from his first wife, Catherine. The Pope refused to grant him his request because of the church's alliance with Spain, and due to the fact that Catherine was a devout Catholic. It was during this time that Lutheranism had begun to lure the populations away from the Roman Catholic Church in various locales, and the Vatican wanted to maintain their strategic stronghold on England. Upon the Pope's refusal to concede to his demands, Henry banned Catholicism in his country and declared himself the head of the new Church of England. He also added to his own coffers by dismantling and selling the abbeys as his own property, and confiscating the religious articles of value for himself. He ultimately and defiantly divorced his first wife, but, in essence, was symbolically divorcing England from Roman Catholicism, for which he was ex-communicated of course. The government of England went from a monarchy to a theocracy overnight, as Henry expected his constituents to follow his lead in leaving Catholicism behind. Under his new "church", reformers of Lutheranism began to speak publically; however, Henry really wanted the church to remain

Catholic in practice but not in name. Under the reign of Henry VIII, and his daughter Mary successively; both Catholics and Protestants were burned as heretics. This religious upheaval left England in a state of turmoil until Henry's daughter, Elizabeth, took the throne. She was a protestant that was unwilling to allow her kingdom to be further affected by the religious commotion of her father's resolution. She had a long and peaceful reign, during which time England stabilized ecclesiastically. The impact of Henry the VIII's religious victory still exists today, as no heir to the throne of England can be a Catholic.

An Egyptian Connection

Their bodies will lie in the street of the great city which is figuratively called Sodom and Egypt, where also their Lord was crucified. (Revelation 11:8)

Almost all bible commentators agree that this is not referring to Jerusalem, but Rome, as Jesus was tried in a Roman court and executed in a Roman fashion. Therefore the connection to Egypt is symbolic. Egypt is mostly referred to as a state of bondage and slavery, however, when this verse is used in connection to Psalm 74:13-14, it is also symbolic of the multi-headed monster in the water. The Psalm does not state a specific number of heads, but one must assume that there are not that many multi-headed monsters and in fact only one is mentioned throughout scripture. Egypt, and specifically Pharaoh, is symbolic of the last world empire beast. God destroyed Pharaoh completely by drowning him in the Red Sea, thereby setting the Israelites free. As with the first three beasts, this monster was more than likely a real creature at one time. In the book of Job, (Job 41:1-34) God is having a conversation with Job and describes a creature that does not physically exist in our world today, yet Job did not act surprised at this information and seemed to understand which creature God was referring to. This creature lived in the sea, had the strength in its jaws to snap iron as if it were straw, red glowing eyes, and breathed fire; God said "Nothing on earth is his equal-a creature without fear".

The book of Revelation goes into great detail about the plagues that are to come upon the earth during the last three and a half years of the tribulation which are directed at the kingdom of the antichrist; the plagues of Egypt were directed at Pharaoh to release the Israelites from captivity. God's Word states that *"I make known the end from the beginning, from ancient times what is still to come."(*Isaiah 46:10) The blueprint for the Exodus from Egypt is going to come upon the whole world, leading to the culmination of the battle of Armageddon and God's deliverance of the Jews and his church from the beast when he is captured and thrown into the lake of fire. The following verses describe the persecution of the saints by the "last beast", the antichrist:

He was given power to make war against the saints and to conquer them. (Revelation 13:7)

The horn was waging war against the saints and defeating them until the Ancient of Days came and pronounced judgment in favor

of the saints of the Most High and the time came when they
possessed the kingdom. (Daniel 7:21)

As the Israelites needed a physical deliverer from the grip of Pharaoh, the Jews and saints will also need a physical deliverance from the power of the antichrist. This will occur with the return of Jesus Christ, when he establishes his kingdom during his millennial reign.

Part III

The Case Against Babylon

Case #1-The Catholic Church Hoards Wealth

Do not store up for yourselves treasures on earth, where moth and rust destroy and thieves break in and steal, rather store up treasures in heaven, where moth and rust do not destroy and thieves do not break in and steal, for where your treasure is, there your heart will be also. (Mathew 6:19)

The Roman Catholic Church is the biggest financial power, wealth accumulator, and property owner in existence. She is a greater possessor of material riches than any other single institution, corporation, bank, giant trust, government or state of the entire globe. The Vatican's treasure of gold in solid bars has been estimated by *UN World Magazine* to amount to several billion dollars. A large bulk stored with the US Federal Reserve, Banks of England and Switzerland, not including real estate, property, stocks, and shares abroad." *Wall Street Journal* states "The Vatican's financial deals in the US alone were so big, that it sold or bought gold in lots of million dollars or more at a time."

The companies that it has invested in are Rothschild of Britain, France, America, Hambros Bank, Credit Suisse London, Zurich, US Morgan Bank, Chase Manhattan, 1st National Bank of New York, and Bankers Trust Company. It also owns share in Gulf Oil, Shell, GM, Bethlehem Steel, GE, IBM, TWA (there are billions in shares alone).

Case #2-The Popes Are Not the Vicars of Christ

Watch out for false prophets. They come to you in sheep's clothing, but inwardly they are ferocious wolves. By their fruit you will recognize them. Do people pick grapes from thorn bushes or figs from thistles? Likewise, every good tree bears good fruit, but a bad tree bears bad fruit. (Matthew 7:15)

The Pope claims to be the "Vicar of Christ", meaning he is equivalent to "Christ on earth". The popes claim they are infallible, yet a review of history should be more than enough to convince anyone that the long line of popes are anything but infallible.

Bad Fruit: Popes from the "Bad Tree" of the Roman Catholic Church

Pope Steven VI - 896-897 AD - He exhumed his predecessor, and put the corpse on trial. The corpse was found guilty and was stripped of its sacred vestments, deprived of its 3 "blessing" fingers of the right hand and eventually the corpse was thrown in the Tiber River.

Pope Benedict IX – 1032-1048 AD - He gave up the Papacy for large sums of money the first time in 1044 AD, was elected again and within a month sold the papacy again for 1,450 pounds of gold. He returned a final time and was forced out by Pope Damascus in 1048 AD. He was described as a demon from hell, feasting on immorality such as homosexuality and bestiality.

Pope Sergius III – 897-911 AD - He ordered the murder of another pope, his reign was known as "The Rise of Pornocracy" or the "Rule of the Harlots", and had an illegitimate son by a prostitute who later became a pope.

Pope John XII – 955-964 AD - One of the worst, he was known to have raped female pilgrims in St. Peters. Emperor Otto I of the Holy Roman Empire leveled charges against him that included converting the Lateran Palace into a brothel, drinking toasts to the devil, and invoking the aid of pagan gods such as Jove and Venus when playing dice.

Pope Alexander VI – 1492-1503 AD - The Rise of the corrupt Borgia family, he had an incestuous relationship with his daughter Lucrezia (some say her son was his), was known for throwing large parties that turned into orgies and pedophilic behavior.

Pope Innocent IV – 1243-1254 AD - He approved the use of torture during the Inquisition to extract confessions of heresy.

Pope Urban VI – 1378-1389 AD - He was prone to outbursts of rage, he elected himself as pope, and began a new papal office in France, and the division in the church became a diplomatic crisis that divided Europe.

Pope John XV – 985-996 AD Split the churches finances among his relatives and was described as "covetous of filthy lucre and corrupt in all his acts."

Pope Innocent III – 1198-1216 AD - Invented and approved the Inquisition

Pope Pius XII - 1939-1958 AD - His office repeatedly refused to publicly denounce the Nazi Regime in the thirties and forties, wanting to remain neutral. Luigi Maglione, a cardinal that served as the Vatican secretary of State under Pope Pius, said the Papacy was "Unable to publicly denounce particular atrocities" (Referring to the Jewish murders). This is still a source of controversy for the Catholic Church today.

Case #3-The Practices of the Catholic Church are Unscriptural

Everything they do is done for men to see: They make their phylacteries wide and the tassels on their garments long; they love the place of honor at banquets and the most important seats in the synagogues; they love to be greeted in the marketplace, and to have men call them "Rabbi", But you are not to be called "Rabbi" for you have only one Master and you are all brothers. And do not call anyone on earth "Father" for you have one Father and he is in heaven. (Mathew 23:5-10)

These are the words of Jesus spoken 2,000 years ago against the *"Religious Institutions"* of Judea. The teachers of Judaism were concerned with their outwardly show of religion by their dress (tassels on their garments), and "phylacteries" wide (a small set of boxes that they strapped to their foreheads and arm that contained verses from the Hebrew bible); the equivalent of wearing a cross around your neck or a religious bumper sticker on your vehicle. They were more concerned with the "show" of their religion than with mercy; God says he is more interested in mercy than sacrifice. Jesus spent a great deal of time addressing the "wrongs" of the religious teachers of the law; what would he say to the priests that are called "Father", the Popes and Cardinals with their "religious attire", and the entire hierarchy of the Papal system that loves to be known and greeted by the adoring enslaved masses?

Case#4-The Defense of the Origins of the Catholic Church Supports Its Destruction

"For by your words you will be acquitted, and by your words you will be condemned." (Mathew 12:37)

The Catholics of the modern church will go to great lengths to defend the "Mother" church. One of the defenses is the supremacy of the apostolic succession of Peter. While trying to defend that Peter was indeed in Rome, they have used the scripture from 1 Peter 5:13 *"She who is in Babylon, chosen together with you, sends you her greetings, and so does my son Mark".*

The commentary from Catholics is that "Babylon" was a code word for Rome, thereby proving that Peter had gone to Rome at some point; however, the biblical verses in Revelation describe Babylon as a harlot (a woman; in scriptures a woman is either the church or the Jewish nation) in red and purple with great wealth, which the Caesars of Rome (iron legs on a male statue) did not have compared to ancient Babylon which was described as having a head of gold or great wealth. Therefore, the harlot in Revelation cannot be ancient Rome. By her own words, she has condemned herself. The ancient Roman Empire fell, but the Roman Catholic Church has not; the day of destruction described in Revelation by John has not yet occurred.

Babylon is still the "Golden Head" of the Vatican in Rome sans beast, and still has a day of destruction ahead. The destruction of Babylon is the "Third Woe" of Revelation.

After this I saw another angel coming down from heaven. He had great authority, and the earth was illuminated by his splendor. With a mighty voice he shouted, "Fallen, Fallen is Babylon the Great! She has become a home for demons, and a haunt for every evil spirit, a haunt for every unclean and detestable bird. For all the nations have drunk the maddening wine of her adulteries. The kings of the earth committed adultery with her, and merchants of the earth grew rich from her excessive luxuries". Come out of her my people, so that you will not share in her sins, so that you will not receive any of her plagues; for her sins are piled up to heaven, and God has remembered her crimes. Give back to her as she has given: pay her back double for what she has done. Mix her a double portion from her own cup. Give her as much torture and grief as the glory and luxury she gave herself. (Revelation 18:1-7)

She sits on many waters – Influence over many people, nations, and languages.

Kings of the earth committed (past tense) adultery with her - To avoid being excommunicated from the Church, the kings would give into the demands of the popes.

Inhabitants of earth were intoxicated with the wine of her adulteries – wine symbolically used at Eucharist Liturgy and adulteries with political powers (mixing of church and state)

Sitting on a scarlet beast in the desert - desert meaning not in power, and beast was the political empire under her reign. She is supposed to sit on many waters, the desert is the time in which she was removed from power.

Dressed in purple and scarlet - colors signify royalty, wealth, colors of the Catholic Church.

Glittering with gold, stones, and pearls – Great wealth, the Vatican treasures

Held a Golden cup in her hand – symbolic of communion with God, golden chalice used in the Eucharist Ceremony

Filled with abominable things – Atrocities committed by the Catholic Church in the name of God

Drunk with the blood of the saints- blood of saints symbolic of the Inquisition, burning of heretics, the crusades, and martyring all those who disagreed with her.

Title on Forehead-Mystery Babylon (secret, from ancient times), Mother of Prostitutes (Mother Church in Rome spawning churches across the globe)

Abominations of the earth – abominations is using Christianity in its purest form as Christ showed from the gospels and perverting it, such as in the "abomination of desolation" described in Daniel, is using the Jewish temple and worshiping another god there. She is accused of worshipping an Idol (the Catholic Church itself) instead of Christ - yet claiming to worship Christ

She sits on seven hills- Rome the city of seven hills, and home of the Vatican.

Part IV
The Inquisition

The 1578 handbook for inquisitors defined the purpose of inquisitorial penalties:

"For punishment does not take place primarily and per se for the correction and good of the person punished, but for the public good in order that others may become terrified and weaned away from the evils they would commit."

A _Heretic_ is defined as: a charge against an individual or group wherein their beliefs challenged Church authority, or were deemed to be inconsistent with orthodox dogma, or an offender against canon law.

The Medieval Institution of the Inquisition

But if we compare the doctrines of the inquisition with those inculcated by the Savior of the world, the folly of the commendations which have been bestowed, will quickly appear manifest If we compare the practice, the same result will follow, and yet both their doctrine and their practice they profess to base upon the mild and merciful precepts, and the divine actions, of the Son of God. -Cyrus Mason

Episcopal Inquisition

The first Inquisition is referred to as the Episcopal Inquisition, and began in 1184 AD under the direction of Pope Innocent III in France to thwart the "freedom of religious thoughts, beliefs, and actions" of Catharism and the Waldensians. Catharism is described as an anti-sacerdotal party in opposition to the Roman Catholic Church protesting against what they perceived to be the moral, spiritual, and political corruption of the church. The Waldensian movement began in Lyon, France in the 1170's as a direct result of the 'Great Schism'; the movement advocated a return to vows of poverty, and preaching of the Gospels as advocated by Jesus and his Disciples. The movement was declared heretical by 1215 AD and became persecuted by church officials. The Duke of Savoy tried to all but exterminate the Waldensians in 1655 AD.

"Anyone who attempts to construe a personal view of God which conflicts with the Church dogma must be burned without pity."   *-Pope Innocent III*

"If you had known what these words mean, "I desire mercy, not sacrifice; you would not have condemned the innocent."   – Jesus Christ (Mathew 12:7)

The Roman Catholic Church is "supposedly built" on the foundation of Peter's confession to Jesus. Jesus asked Peter a question, the question merits freedom of religious thought. *"But what about you?"* he asked. *"Who do you say I am?"* Simon Peter answered, *"You are the Christ, the Son of the living God."* (Mathew 16:15)

The leading question asked by Jesus followed by Peter's response is indicative of how each individual comes willingly to Christ; through a personal view of God.

The Cathar heresy was a major challenge to the Roman Catholic Church. The Cathars rejected the Roman Catholic, the entire church structure. They developed an alternative religion that attracted many adherents in that period, which is why the Cathar heresy above all occasioned the founding of the inquisition. Thirteenth century was at a high point of its power and influence. The popes of that period were very powerful and they interfered very broadly in the affairs of secular monarchies. They had tremendous power over religious orders and very significant authority over the appointment of bishops. It was a very powerful church but it was also a church that was troubled by corruption. It was now a movement that had brick and mortar churches and episcopal hierarchy and an elaborate bureaucracy and it collected tax money from all over Europe. Some of its prelates lived in great splendor; they were like feudal lords themselves. In so far as the Church was enmeshed in the world the radical rejection of the world by the Cathars posed an enormous threat. Referring to Western Europe, the world of Christendom was a world of monarchies that were developing, but were as yet poorly organized. The papacy itself was also a monarchy, having the papal state in central Italy; the pope ruling as a secular ruler with about a third of Italy under his direct control. Every sovereign took upon himself the protection of the Roman Catholic Church in the twelfth and thirteenth centuries. Europe was completely Roman Catholic. A heretical movement therefore in seeking to undermine Roman Catholicism also could be seen as a direct threat to the State. Heresy, given the political theory of the middle Ages, could easily be equated with treason as we would understand it; in other words, a betrayal of government and society - simply because there was a total identification between religious belief and loyalty to the sovereign. Catharism becomes the most important of the 13th century heresies, in part because of the support of the lesser nobility, in part because it struck a responsive chord among so many people in Medieval Europe in terms of their own apprehensions and insecurities about the Church and their feelings that the Church needed to be reformed or changed or maybe itself was corrupt.

-Dr. Stephen Haliczer, Northern Illinois University

Papal Inquisition

The inquisition was established, the scourge of the world, and the most corrupt engine ever wielded. - Cyrus Mason

The second wave of the Inquisition is known as the Papal Inquisition which began in the 1230's and lasted until the late nineteenth century. It was during this stage of the Inquisition that a formal tribunal for the Inquisitions was established, along with an appointed 'Grand Inquisitor'. By 1256 AD, Inquisitors were given absolution if they used instruments of torture; many of the devices were engraved with "Glory be to God." The minor penances for the accused, depending on the level of heresy involved, could be pilgrimages, public scourging, fines, confiscation of property with the disinheriting of the accused's heirs, or outright ex-communication. For those unlucky enough to find themselves in the dungeon awaiting their fate at the hands of the Inquisitor could be any of the following:

The Rack-more popular during the Spanish Inquisition; the body after tying the extremities on the rack, would be pulled out of its joints.

The Stocks-after locking the head and arms into the contraption, the feet of the accused would be lathered with grease while standing on a surface heated by flames underneath, the feet would literally be fried.

Water Torture-up to eight gallons of water would be poured down a victims' throat distending the abdomen until it burst.

Heretics Fork-a utensil with fork tines on each end would be strapped under an accused chin, the victim would be unable to relax their head as the tines would dig into the chin and chest area.

The Branks-a metal facial mask with a spiked mouth depressor, this would commonly be used even by husbands on housewives should she disobey and was fully approved by the church.

Several other devices, each more heinous than the last included The Wheel, The Pear, Hanging Cages, Breast Ripper, Head Crusher, Iron Maiden, The Strappado, The Boots, and The Judas Cradle.

Punishments were sentenced by the tribunal in the Catholic Church, and the individual would be remanded to secular authorities to have the punishment meted.

"The torturers took high advantage of positions of authority to indulge in the most pornographic sessions of sexual control over their victims."- Ann Barstow

During the Papal Inquisition, any ruler (King or Prince) refusing to purge his land of heretics by order of the Pope would be ex-communicated and his country would be seized by the Catholics who, after fulfilling their mission would be given the same indulgence as the Crusaders received. Allegiance to the Church only was required –God was left out of the equation. The Bible was, of course, preserved during the five hundred plus years of the Inquisitions, as it was never used; and more than likely sat on a shelf collecting dust in the Papal library. The Inquisitions were so effective, according to the Church, that the Council of Toulouse in 1229 AD adopted a number of canons tending to give permanent character to the Inquisition as a "permanent institution."

The persecution of witchcraft also enabled the Church to prolong the profitability of the Inquisition. The Inquisition had left regions so economically destitute, that the Inquisitor, Eymeric, complained, *"In our days there are no more rich heretics...it is a pity that so salutary an institution as ours should be so uncertain of its future."*

Pope Gregory IX urged one of the Inquisitors, Conrad of Marburg in Germany, to *"not so much punish the wicked, but hurt the innocent with fear."* This particular Inquisitor was quoted as stating, *"I would gladly burn a hundred innocent if there was one guilty among them."*

The Church was in the grip of madness and was being used as a tool of Satan. Instead of a light to the world, it had become an all-consuming darkness which lasted over half a millennia; during which time the general population of Europe lived in a level of fear and anxiety that no longer exists anywhere in the world.

The Spanish Inquisition began in 1480 AD in the districts of Seville, Castile, and Aragon, and was unique from the Papal Inquisition in that it was established by the monarchy itself, King Ferdinand and Queen Isabella. By this time, the Dominicans were in charge of the Inquisitions of the Papacy, and upon request from the Spanish crown, commenced in Spain as well. The main idea in Spain was to round up the wealthiest heretics, as their confiscated property would be divided between the crown and the Dominicans. The first "auto de facto" (Act of faith) occurred in 1480 in the district of Seville. Huge public burnings took place in Spain on commencement of the Inquisition of those who would not accept the Catholic faith, which were mainly Jews and Muslims. Likewise, the Portuguese Inquisition which lasted from 1536 to 1821 targeted Sephardic Jews for conversion.

The last phase of the European Inquisitions was the Roman Inquisition in Italy, which began in 1542 and endured until 1860. It was this Inquisition that found Galileo guilty on charges of heresy, when they deemed his Heliocentric Theory as against the views of the Church, for which he was sentenced to lifetime house arrest.

The Catholic supporters of the modern Roman Church and the Papacy are supporting the past crimes committed by this religious institution. For an Institution that denies most of its crimes and has not so much as paid restitution is nothing more than a fugitive. A 'Father William' wrote an article trying to excuse his church of the crimes committed by using a comparison of the secular corporal punishments used throughout Europe during the times of the Inquisition. In that statement, he is saying that there is no difference between the Church and secular governments, thereby condoning the atrocities committed by the Roman Church and absolving them of any wrongdoing. These 'supporters' claim that Protestants are "catholic bashing" when addressing the history of the Roman Church as *that was in the past, the church is reformed now*. If her crimes were absolved by God, then she would not be on God's "destruction" list. When reading the words of scriptures, and especially the words of Jesus, one can know that Jesus never advocated violence, only love. By defending the Catholic Church, they are partaking of her crimes.

"You will be ever hearing but never understand; you will be ever seeing but never perceiving, For this people's heart has become calloused; they hardly hear with their ears, and they have closed their eyes. Otherwise they might see with their eyes, hear with their ears, understand with their hearts and turn, and I would heal them" (Mathew 13:14-15)

In Revelation, the angel tells John that "Mystery Babylon" is guilty of all those who have died in the earth. The blood of all the righteous was spilled by the "religious institutions of Mystery Babylon". The meaning to that mysterious proclamation is found in Mathew; Jesus is addressing the Pharisees which are none other than 'religious teachers of the law' irrespective of their Jewish heritage.

"You snakes! You brood of vipers! How will you escape being condemned to hell? Therefore I am sending you prophets and wise men and teachers. Some of them you will kill and crucify; others you will flog in your synagogues and pursue from town to town. And so upon you will come all the righteous blood that has been shed on earth, from the blood of righteous Abel, to the blood of Zechariah, son of Berekiah, whom you murdered between the temple and the altar. I tell you the truth; all this will come upon this generation. (Mathew 23:33-36)

God showed great compassion on the city of Nineveh to send a prophet to them and to spare them from destruction, yet Jesus blasts the religious teachers of the law of his own countrymen, and tells them they are responsible for all the righteous blood shed on earth. The reason is found in the verses below:

But Nineveh has more than a hundred and twenty thousand people who cannot tell their right hand from their left and many cattle as well. (Jonah 4:11)

Not many of you should presume to be teachers, my brothers, because you know that we who teach will be judged more strictly. (James 2:3)

The sheep are guided by a shepherd, if the shepherd leads the sheep astray, they are lost, but not by their own doing. The religious institutions of Judea and the Medieval Roman Catholic Church had a few similarities. They killed those who tried to warn them that they were in error, and they burdened their congregations with unnecessary rules, restrictions and regulations in order to obtain salvation.

Destruction of Babylon-The Seventh Bowl

The woman you saw is the great city that rules over the kings of the earth. (Revelation 17:18)

The angel is speaking to John in present tense at this point; using the word "*is*" the great city. The great city that ruled over the kings of the earth was Rome, which after the empire fell, moved to the Roman Catholic Church. John wrote many parts of Revelation in coded references that the church would understand, yet a Roman confiscating the material would not.

The seventh angel poured out his bowl into the air, and out the temple came a loud voice from the throne saying, "It is done!" Then there came flashes of lightning, rumblings, peals of thunder and a severe earthquake. No earthquake like it has ever occurred since man has been on earth, so tremendous was the quake. The great city split into three parts, and the cities of the nations collapsed. God remembered Babylon the Great and gave her the cup filled with the wine of the fury of his wrath.
(Revelation 16:17-19)

Rome will be devastated by this earthquake; the city along with Vatican City will be split into three parts. Seven thousand people will die in Rome as a result of this quake.

When they see the smoke of her burning, they will exclaim, 'Was there ever a city like this great city?' (Revelation 18:18)

At that very hour there was a severe earthquake and a tenth of the city collapsed. Seven thousand people were killed in the earthquake, and the survivors were terrified and gave glory to the God of Heaven. (Revelation 11:13)

God sends two witnesses to preach on the earth during three and one half years of the tribulation. These two witnesses preach in Rome for a specific reason; just as God sent Jonah to preach to Nineveh before its destruction, he is sending a warning to the inhabitants of Rome. God wants his children to come out of Rome and Vatican City before it is destroyed.

These men have power to shut up the sky so that it will not rain during the time they are prophesying; and they have power to turn the waters into blood and to strike the earth with every kind of plague as often as they want. (Revelation 11:6)

The same power used by Elijah and Moses are bestowed on these two prophets. Jesus predicted their return, and these two witnesses perish at the hands of the antichrist, yet they are raised from the dead.

Jesus replied, "To be sure, Elijah comes and will restore all things. But I tell you, Elijah has already come and they did not recognize him, but have done to him everything they wished. In the same way the Son of Man is going to suffer at their hands." (Matthew 17:11-12)

Now when they have finished their testimony, the beast that comes up from the Abyss will attack them, and overpower and kill them. Their bodies will lie in the street of the great city, which is figuratively called Sodom and Egypt, where also their Lord was crucified. For three and a half days men from every people tribe language and nation will gaze on their bodies and refuse them burial. The inhabitants of the earth will gloat over them and will celebrate by sending each other gifts, because these two prophets had tormented those who live on the earth. (Revelation 11:7-10)

The Lord raised them from the dead after three and a half days, and it terrified the viewing audience; I'm sure every news camera on earth will be pointed at their bodies. The people on earth whose names are not written in the book of life will view them as outsiders to planet earth; they will view them as "not quite human" because of the damage they cause and will be glad when they're killed. That will be the sad state of affairs during the last days, the majority of the earth's population will not understand what is happening. Any person that authors a book on bible prophecy usually has a specific reason for doing so; they have information to share about a specific view on a biblical subject. Regardless of their viewpoint, at some point they reflect on how very tragic the outcome is for the millions of lives that will be lost in the last days.

With such violence the great city of Babylon will be thrown down, never to be found again. (Revelation 18:21)

The two witnesses that appear are the last two prophets that will emerge on earth before the return of Jesus and their arrival is a warning for everyone to repent or be eternally lost. The two witnesses preach, are killed and resurrected in spiritual Babylon, and then "The Great Harlot" is destroyed.

Animal Planet

In my vision at night, I looked and there before me were
the four winds of heaven churning up the great sea.
Four great beasts, each different from the others, came
up out of the sea. – Daniel 7:2

Chapter 3

✟

Daniel contains more key prophecies of the end times than any other book in the Bible with the exception of Revelation, and also relates the most specific prophecies pertaining to the actions of the coming antichrist. Daniel also had many visions and dreams concerning the world kingdoms yet to come. In the last chapter we examined the dream that King Nebuchadnezzar had of a statue made of metal and discussed the kingdoms that it represented. Daniel had many dreams and visions as well; the most notably debated by scholars and theologians is the vision of the four beasts rising up from the sea. Some scholars feel this is an historic vision fulfilled in the first four empires, while others, including the views expressed in this chapter, interpret it as a pre Elizabethan-era vision which began during the reign of Henry the VIII. This book expresses the understanding that most of the beast empires occurred or were finalized prophetically directly before and during the twentieth century.

In the first year of King Belshazzar of Babylon, Daniel had a dream, and visions passed through his mind as he was lying on his bed. He wrote down the substance of his dream. In my vision at night I looked, and there before me were the four winds of heaven churning up the great sea. Four great beasts, each different from the other, came up out of the sea. The first was like a lion, and it had the wings of an eagle. I watched until its wings were torn off and it was lifted from the ground so that it stood on two feet like a man, and the heart of a man was given to it. And there before me was a second beast, which looked like a bear. It was raised up on one of its sides and it had three ribs in its mouth between its teeth. It was told "get up and eat your fill of flesh!" After that, I looked, and there before me was another beast, one that looked like a leopard. And on its back it had four wings like those of a bird. This beast had four heads and it was given authority to rule. After that, in my vision at night I looked and there before me was a fourth beast-terrifying and frightening and very powerful. It had large iron teeth: it crushed and devoured its victims and trampled underfoot whatever was left. It was different from all the former beasts, and it had ten horns. (Daniel 7:1-7)

These verses were first interpreted by bible scholars before 1900 AD. The men who translated the bible from the King James Version into other modern versions took these verses to be symbolic of the first four kingdoms that were indicated by the metal statue. This is one of the most widely misinterpreted prophecies by pastors and biblical scholars, including prophecy pioneers such as C.I. Scofield. When this particular chapter was interpreted, most events had not yet occurred. Scofield was interpreting these and many other scriptures around the time of the civil war in America. The interpreters of these prophecies a century or more ago did not have the necessary details because they had not lived through the twentieth century.

Modern theologians interpret this chapter by simply picking up where Scofield and others left off without fully examining the scriptures. Chapter seven of Daniel is one of the most profound prophecies for the twentieth century and has been overlooked by a majority of bible prophecy contemporaries. By not thoroughly probing the scriptures, they have made erroneous conclusions as to the origins of the four beasts. We will examine these scriptures verse by verse to ascertain that these prophecies were not fulfilled in antiquity but into the twentieth and now the twenty-first century.

In the first year of King Belshazzar of Babylon, Daniel had a dream, and visions passed through his mind as he was lying on his bed. He wrote down the substance of his dream. (Daniel 7:1)

When Daniel had this dream, he was still in exile in Babylon, however, King Nebuchadnezzar was dead and King Belshazzar was on the throne. This is an important verse; King Nebuchadnezzar had the original dream of the metal statue, but it was under a new king that Daniel received this vision. In the dream of the statue, God told King Nebuchadnezzar that he was the head of gold. At this point I want to reiterate that God is not the author of confusion. (1 Corinthians 14:33)

There would have been no need for God to give Daniel a second dream of the first four empires again, there is no logic for this and God is logical as he created logic. A lot of scholars consider these verses to be God confirming the dream of the statue, however; God's word is his confirmation and he had already given Daniel the original interpretation of the statue dream. Biblical scholars have run into an illogical "stumbling block" to discern why Daniel saw three beasts rise from the sea which they have interpreted as the old Babylon, Mede-Persian, and Grecian empires and then have to jump forward several millennia to interpret the fourth beast that follows, which is the beast under the antichrist. When God wants to emphasize something, it is obvious; such as in (Mathew 24:15) Jesus referred to the *"abomination that causes desolation spoken of by the prophet Daniel"*. In Daniel that phrase is repeated four separate times: (Daniel 8:11-13, 9:27, 11:31, and 12:11)

 That is God's method of repetition and it doesn't create confusion, because he wants average people to read His Word and understand it clearly.

In my vision at night I looked, and there before me were the four winds of heaven churning up the great sea. (Daniel 7:2)

The four winds of heaven were indicative of the compass position of north, south, east and west; in other words it is the four corners of the earth and is not geographically confined to one continent. The great sea represents many gentile nations, and languages. It is used in the book of Revelation referring to the great prostitute that is sitting on many waters.

Four great beasts, each different from the other, came up out of the sea. (Daniel 7:3)

The four beasts were each different from another. As we explained in a previous chapter, each of those kingdoms of the statue resembled the one prior as they were all connected to the same head. The beasts represent new kingdoms and governments after Rome ceased to be a kingdom. "Coming up out of the great sea" indicates globally, as opposed to the kingdoms of the statue that were somewhat confined to the Middle East and Eastern Europe.

Only a rudimentary understanding of world affairs is needed to perceive the identity of the first two beasts and the modern nations they symbolize, a lion and bear. It is important in understanding this prophecy, that all of the book of Daniel must be taken into account. Consider the following verse:

But you Daniel close up and seal the words of the scroll until the time of the end. Many will go here and there to increase knowledge. (Daniel 12:4)

Here, the angel gave an explanation as to why some of these prophecies were misinterpreted prior to 1948; the "words" of the prophecy were sealed. When considering the almost 6000 years we have spent on the earth, using only fire for cooking, light and heating; the explosion of knowledge in the twentieth century is the words of that prophecy coming to pass or being unsealed. With the turn of the previous century came electricity and the first automobile; sixty years later, the first man landed on the moon. The landing on the moon inspired the words, "One small step for man; one giant leap for mankind"; and also a giant leap in the increase of knowledge. Every single decade of the last century saw a new invention; the further into the future mankind goes, the more our knowledge increases. The words of the prophecy "*the* time of the end" and "knowledge shall increase" are interwoven.

The renaissance of the 1600's gave birth to some of the most innovative thinkers of that millennium, yet their knowledge was trampled on and labeled as "heresy" under the rule of the Roman Catholic Church; the risk of saying the earth was round, or the sun doesn't revolve around our planet, would have led to being beheaded, burned at the stake, or at the least, being arrested or excommunicated.

Sir Isaac Newton, an English scientist and mathematician, was one of the most interesting of the 'Renaissance Era' "innovative thinkers". He is famous for his laws of gravity and motion among other scientific discoveries, however, it was his unpublished work referred to as the 'Portsmouth Papers', which were made known to the general public in 2003, that raised eyebrows in modern theological circles. He was known as an insightful theologian in his time, but it was his predictions, made by mathematical computations while studying Daniel and Revelation, that were widely unknown during his lifetime. The most intriguing of his predictions stated that Jesus Christ would not return, nor would the apocalypse occur before the year 2060. His calculations included the 1260, 1290, 1335 and 2300 day for year substitution found in a discourse in Daniel. He stated that he had not made the prediction to set a date, but rather, because he disliked individuals who were date-setting for sensational value at that time. He also extensively researched the Temple of Solomon, believing it was designed by divine guidance. He felt that the blueprint of the temple also represented a "time-frame" chronology of Hebrew history. Some of his beliefs were considered occultic in his time and would have been deemed as heresy to the Church of England. He withheld much of his theological beliefs from peers, knowing that should his beliefs be discovered, he could incur loss of property, status, or even death.

Another innovative thinker during the Renaissance was Galileo Galilei, an Italian astronomer, physicist, mathematician, and philosopher. He is considered the "Father of Modern Observational Astronomy, Physics, and Science". His scientific observations over the 'Theory of Heliocentrism' (earth revolves around the sun) clashed with the views of the Roman Catholic Church. He was brought before the Roman Inquisition in 1615 where he was found suspect of heresy, and put under house arrest for the duration of his life. During the Age of Enlightenment, the Roman Catholic Church snuffed out knowledge and life for three reasons; fear of the unknown, power, and ignorance. The Catholic Church continued to remain in darkness while the rest of the world began to emerge from the suffocating tyranny and oppression inflicted by the 'Vicar of Christ' under the cloak of "religion". America offered relief to those fleeing from the religious persecution of Europe, and the many beasts she harbored during the dark ages.

Lion

The first was like a lion, and it had the wings of an eagle. I watched until its wings were torn off and it was lifted from the ground so that it stood on two feet like a man, and the heart of a man was given to it. (Daniel 7:4)

The lion was and still is the symbol of Great Britain and the symbol of a monarchy. Her eagle's wings were the tiny colony in the Americas. Those wings were ripped off in 1776 when America declared her independence and won the Revolutionary War. Wings symbolize movement or expansion prophetically, Britain ruled the colonies in America and the wings were attached until America declared her own freedom from the crown of Great Britain. The saying of "the sun never set on the British empire" was true; Great Britain had the largest empire in history. Her empire spanned the globe, and it was far larger than the Roman Empire ever was. Yet only the symbol of America's wings were attached to her; the reason for this is the next part of the verse, "it was lifted off the ground and stood on two feet like a man, and the heart of a man was given to it". After America declared her independence, Great Britain began to govern in the interest of the people under her control instead of like a beast. A beast is an empire, caring only for power and expansion, Britain began dissimilating her colonies and her power began to wane so much in that by World War II, Great Britain was waiting on America to take control.

Bear

World War II brings us to the next beast:

And there before me was a second beast, which looked like a bear. It was raised up on one of its sides and it had three ribs in its mouth between its teeth. It was told "get up and eat your fill of flesh!" (Daniel 7:5)

A bear is Russia's national personification; it was called a Russian Bear as far back as 1817 during *"The Great Game",* between the British Lion, the Russian Bear, and the Persian Cat. The Russian empire had tried to expand beyond its borders and take over parts of the British Empire in central Asia, thereby taking away Great Britain's crown jewel, India. The story goes 'the Lion said to the bear, "What are you doing playing with my little cat?" the cat meaning Persia (Iraq). During this time Russia had gone to war with Japan which was short-lived, but Russia eventually succeeded during World War II. The bear raised up on its side (which would have been towards the east) with three ribs in its mouth was the defeat of Germany, Italy, and Japan in 1945. It was allowed to feast upon the nations that had troubled it since the early 1800's. From the turn of the century until 1945 Russia had been allies with the west, but its refusal to pull out troops in Iran caused the beginning of the cold war between Russia and the U.S. After 46 years the Soviet Union collapsed on itself in 1991 and the iron curtain fell due to internal turmoil, shortages of food, and lack of common commodities for the public. Like bears, Russia is hibernating, repairing itself, and waiting for the time to eat its fill of flesh again. This bear beast has been incorrectly identified as the Mede/Persian Empire by many scholars, who believe it to be the same empire as the silver chest and arms of the statue. There is proof in the bible that the two are not the same.

I looked up, and there before me was a ram with two horns, standing beside the canal, and the horns were long. One of the horns was longer than the other but grew up later. (Daniel 8: 3)

The two horned ram that you saw represents the kings of Media and Persia. (Daniel 8:20)

In the ancient world, as now, only one animal can represent a nation or kingdom at a time, Mede/Persia (Modern Iran/Iraq) cannot be a ram and a bear, it would create confusion and an absence of logic. The bear was an animal of a future kingdom unknown at the time of Daniel's writing. The Mede/Persian Empire was defeated by, and incorporated into Greece which was identified as a shaggy goat. Since the bear cannot represent Mede/Persia, then the lion cannot represent Babylon. The proof in the preceding verses should prompt the reader to look for another kingdom as the bear's identity.

A recent article in Reuters indicated that Russia has recently threatened a new cold- war-style arms race with Washington, due to the US expansion of its missile defense program in Europe. Russia stated that the balance of power would be unequaled giving the US hegemony should Washington continue on the current path. In a panel talk at London's Royal United Services Institute Think Tank, Dmitry Rogozin said "The *Russian bear* sits in its lair and the NATO huntsman comes to his house and asks him to come hunt the rabbit...The bear asks "Why do your rifles have the caliber to hunt the bear instead of the rabbit?"

The world still recognizes the bear as a symbol of Russia, and realizes it is in hibernation.

Leopard

After that, I looked, and there before me was another beast, one that looked like a leopard. And on its back it had four wings like those of a bird. This beast had four heads and it was given authority to rule. (Daniel 7:6)

Depicted here is a picture of a four headed leopard with wings on its back. As we saw with the lion, wings are movement and/or expansion, and these wings remain attached to the body of the leopard. The heads of the leopard denote succession of rulers within a particular kingdom, as in a certain period of time they would have "passed down or inherited their rule of this kingdom." The four wings are movement of this kingdom by either expansion or another nation adopting this type of ruler ship as well. As with all the other beasts, this kingdom would have had the spotlight after Russia began its decline, which began in 1950 with the start of the cold war; just as Russia did not increase until after Great Britain began its decline. England and Russia have continued to exist, and neither country had to be conquered. The same applies to this new empire. We know from scrutinizing the Russian bear that the Great game was played with Iraq, which was called the Persian cat. This third beast applies to almost the entire Middle East and some parts of Africa as well but its original country of birth was Saudi Arabia. The leopard represents the historical Muslim Empires of Islam as "heads" and present Islamic states as its "wings" in a theocracy, which is a government that rules by adhering to the laws of its religion. Islam is the main religion of the Middle East and is the identity of the leopard. The majority of the countries of the Middle East have been under the control of successive dynasties since 661 AD, after the formation of Islam as a religion. The rule of the "heads" ended in 1922 when Great Britain conquered and disbanded the Ottoman Empire. The world in the nineteenth century understood which countries the beasts symbolized during "The Great Game", a lion, bear, and a cat playing together.

The four heads, which denotes the succession of this rule, began after Islam was established in Saudi Arabia. The four ruling dynasties started from the time of Mohammed with the Umayyad Dynasty in 661 AD and lasted until 1922 when Great Britain conquered the Ottoman Empire at the end of World War I.

The consecutive dynasties or the "heads" were:

Umayyad	**(661-750 AD)**
Abbasid	**(750-1258 AD)**
Fatimad	**(910-1269 AD)**
Ottoman	**(1451-1922 AD)**

The leopard was actually the first of these beasts; however, it did not come into existence in accordance to the prophecy until 2001, after all the wings were in place. When the first dynasty of Islam was formed, the leopard only had its first head in power; with each successive dynasty came power to another head until 1922, when the ultimate Ottoman dynasty came to an end. The four wings that are attached to the leopard are locations or countries, other than Saudi Arabia, where the theocracy of Islam has been established as the official form of government. The first nation to declare itself an Islamic state was Pakistan in 1956. It was followed by Mauritania in 1958, Iran in 1979, and Afghanistan in 2001.

Nations that have declared themselves an Islamic State:

Pakistan	**1956**
Mauritania	**1958**
Iran	**1979**
Afghanistan	**2001**

It was entirely impossible to understand this prophecy of the leopard prior to 1956. Until these nations declared themselves Islamic states there was no way to identify the wings of the leopard.

The leopard has, like the bear, been wrongly identified as Alexander the Great and the Empire of Greece. There is again biblical proof that it is not:

Suddenly a goat with a prominent horn between his eyes came from the west, crossing the whole earth without touching the ground. (Daniel 8:5)

The shaggy goat is the king of Greece and the large horn between his eyes is the first king. The four horns that replaced the one that was broken off represent four kingdoms that will emerge from his nation but will not have the same power. (Daniel 8:21)

It is impossible for the kingdom of Greece to be a goat and a leopard at the same time.

The entire vision Daniel had of the four beasts was **the last four empires of the world**, because the book was to be sealed shut until the time of the end. The span of time between the last empire of the statue (Rome), and the first beast empire (Great Britain) is the exact timeframe of the rule of the Roman Catholic Church.

History of the Great Deception

Islam began in 586 under the teachings of a false prophet named Mohammed in Mecca, Saudi Arabia. He was referred to as a false prophet by early Christian and Jewish Byzantine writers throughout Judea during that time. Christianity was actually the accelerant for Mohammed to propagate his new found religion across Saudi Arabia. The story of Mohammed and Islam began when Christianity began to spread throughout the Middle East. His father was a merchant, and Mohammed traveled with him for trading. While traveling by caravan on a routine business trip, he came across a Christian monk; the monk undoubtedly shared his faith and the story of Christ with him. Mohammed took this information and combined it with the story of Abraham and Ishmael to create Islam. The religion of Islam speaks to an Arabs' pride; instead of being the decedents of the child who had been cast out, they were now the chosen children of their God "Allah". It was said that he spent much time alone in caves close to his home in meditation and prayer in the early days of Islam, and that he was visited by angels who ministered to him. If he had contact with celestial beings, it was of demonic origins that wanted to spread a false, hate-filled religion that would conflict with Christianity. This is how Satan has sown "weeds" into the fields of "wheat" in the world. Although the Crusades of the Roman Catholic Church were inherently evil and the cause of much bloodshed, God used the crusades to slow the growth of Islam. Islam would have covered all of Europe centuries ago except that God's timing did not allow it to happen until this age, *the time of the end.*

Arabs in pre-Islamic Arabia were, and still are, pagans; they had religious shrines as did many other pagan cultures in the Middle East. One shrine in particular still exists in Mecca that Muslims pilgrimage to yearly. The shrine in Mecca was in use for a pagan religion before the birth of Islam, and was simply converted as Arabs continued to pilgrimage after Islam was established. *The History Channel* made a very informative documentary of the shrine in Mecca that displayed thousands of Muslims surrounding the tiny shrine. There is a black stone encased on the shrine, this stone was a part of the ancient pagan shrine as well; it has been in use for several millennia. The same type of occurrence happened within the Roman Catholic Church, the parishioners were unwilling to give up idol worship within Christianity, and many still wanted a "visual aid" to bow down to. The solution for the early Catholic fathers was to change the names on the pagan statues in Rome and Greece from pagan god names to Christian ones, for instance, the god "Jupiter" became "Peter", and the goddess "Isis" to "Mary". This method of incorporating the old with the new insured an easier transition for the new adherents of Islam. The truth of the story of the Arabic peoples has its origins in their patriarchal father, Ishmael. While waiting for God's promise of a child through Sarah; Abraham, through Sarah's urging, had a child through Sarah's Egyptian maidservant Hagar. She bore him a son, but later, when Sarah had her child of promise, Isaac, she became jealous and did not want Ishmael to share in Isaac's inheritance. Hagar and her son were banished from their home. Hagar went to the wilderness and upon searching for water and couldn't find any, she gave up hope thinking her child would die. God spoke to her and told her that he would bless Ishmael as well and that ***"he would become a great nation and a father of twelve rulers"*** (Genesis 17: 20). Ishmael's nation of twelve "rulers" comprises the modern Islamic Middle East: Bahrain, Kuwait, Lebanon, Oman, Qatar, Yemen, United Arab Emirates, Syria, Turkey, Iran, Iraq, and Saudi Arabia.

Palestine is not included due to the fact that it was not referred to as "Palestine" until the Roman Emperor

Hadrian renamed Judea, and it would entail the lands that were given in covenant to Israel. The same reasoning applies to Jordan as biblically the land belongs to the Israelites.

God also told Hagar that *"Ishmael will be a wild donkey of a man, his hand will be against everyone and everyone's hand against him; he will live in hostility toward all his brothers."* (Genesis 16:12)

That verse verbatim is almost the Arab and Islamic creed, as that is exactly how they have lived. They fight with all their Arabic brothers and their families, even to execute honor killings against their own mothers, sisters and daughters; unless they unite to fight against a foreign enemy such as the U.S. or Israel.

After identifying the leopard, one only has to watch current events and realize which nations are gaining the most attention. After Great Britain conquered and disbanded the Ottoman Empire in 1922, the Arab world had to find its new identity. Muslims found themselves in a country that had been renamed, rezoned, and struggling to form a new government. Famines hit some Arabic countries hard during the twenties; Iran lost a large majority of its population to starvation. Other Middle Eastern countries have been war ravaged with a very slow recovery, while some have recently found a new freedom from harsh dictatorships occurring in many Middle Eastern countries as a result of "The Arab Spring". The greatest commodity of the Middle East is crude oil, and it was not discovered until the twenties. Certain countries such as Kuwait and Saudi Arabia found themselves very wealthy seemingly overnight.

The attention most westerners give to the Middle East, however, has to do with terrorism; either globally, or within the Middle East itself. Car bombs, hijackings, and suicide bombers are some new phrases that began around the seventies and have become more frequent in the world we now live in; such violent activities have become weekly news reports from that part of the globe. The reason behind the violence is the religion of Islam in itself; the claims of Islam are a religion of peace and love, and yet it propagates violence through Shari'ah law using verses from much of the Qur'an to support violence and bloodshed. In Iran, prior to 1979, the Shah was an ally of the US; the country proliferated in freedoms such as democracy, and women enjoyed the same privileges held by their American counterparts. After the installment of the Ayatollah in 1979, human rights, especially women's, have been extinguished and the worst atrocities are committed there under the guise of religion. It is the "Adam Effect", the overemphasized belief of the superiority of men and the inferiority of women, that has occurred in that country over the last 34 years, in that the people of the region are still of the same ethnicity, however, the laws have changed under the widespread religious Islamic ideology. Women in Islamic countries are basically treated as human garbage, they are called "property", however, true property such as cattle or belongings are treated with more care by most Muslim men.

Many theories still abound as to the identity of the leopard by some who do not adhere to the traditional eschatology view of the leopard symbolism representing ancient Greece; one theory is that it represents Germany and a Fourth Reich to manifest. With the exception of the four "heads", this is an impossible scenario leaving no reasonable explanation for the wings as movement of the Reichs, as they have always been located in Germany, and the fact that Germany has never been identified with a "cat". Also, like the other beasts, Germany would have needed to regain its power as a "Fourth Reich" following Russia's decline; however Germany was recovering from World War II for years afterward. It is not a coincidence that Hitler called his "hideout" the 'Wolf's Lair'. If any animal described Germany, it would be the wolf. Hitler systematically annihilated the "sheep" of Israel; Jesus told his apostles he was *"sending them out as sheep among wolves"* (Mathew 10:16).

Muslims, like orthodox Jews, are awaiting a messiah. The fourth "terrifying" beast has the body of a leopard; therefore, the reader can recognize the 'leopard' as referring to the 'body or nation of Islam'. They will believe the antichrist is their awaited messiah or "Mahdi", the 12th Imam. When reading Islamic eschatology, it has been intertwined so much with Christianity that it is almost verbatim of some parts of Revelation regarding the return of Jesus Christ. That is the work of the enemy; a religion created to be supposedly equal to or greater than Christianity, and a "god" holier than the God of the bible, in which Christians are considered inferior to Muslims. Jesus spoke of a parable of 'the wheat and the tares' in which the enemy sowed weeds amongst the wheat; this is the visual result of that happening in the world. The Islamic culture of the Middle East is the most difficult to penetrate with the Gospel of Christ because Muslims already understand much of Christianity and feel their Islamic beliefs are superior.

Some characteristics of the leopard are its stealth and speed as a predator, and its spots used as camouflage to conceal itself from prey, sometimes hiding amongst its prey without its presence known.

Islamic Fundamentalism is predicated as a predatory religion, as it pronounces anyone of another faith an infidel, and promises 'jihad' or holy war against all infidels. A decade ago, the leaders of our country realized the threats our enemies posed to our nation and took appropriate measures to insure national security; if the preceding administration had not set the wheels in motion to capture the responsible party for the terrorist attack in New York, Osama Bin Laden would still be at large. Our current administration is either completely ignorant of these facts or is more concerned with being politically correct. We now have the type of weak leadership in America that would enable the fourth beast to rise to power by handing over the reins of our country in appeasement. Obama's current relationship to Israel is civil at best. He appears to be a leader that does not know his allies from his enemies, and has in the past term spread open arms to nations that despise American culture, values, freedoms, and way of life. He seems to place his personal opinion, based on his former interaction in foreign nations as a civilian and personal socialist agenda above the welfare of the nation that he presides over. During President Obama's past term in office, our government has taken a different attitude towards the factions that have been in the past acknowledged as our enemies. The leadership in America has recently taken great strides in bowing to pressure in relation to issues regarding Islam and it leaves a large majority of the American population wondering why; when we still have a constitution that upholds the separation of church and state. That particular constitutional amendment is not solely applied to Christianity, yet it is the morally held position of Christians that seem to undergo continuous attacks in the courts and media. The agenda of the current administration appears to be attempting to desensitize the American public to the values of America as acknowledged by our founding fathers, while embracing a much larger position; one that is global.

Radical Islam & Homegrown Terrorists

The Clarion Project is a website that has well documented the rise of Islamic Fundamentalism, as well as radical Islam, across the globe. They have documented, through their website, much of the terrorist activities that are occurring as a result of radical Islam. Much of the following information has been garnered from their website (theclarionproject.org).

Since the terrorist's attacks of September 11th, 2001; the US has prevented at least thirty-one attacks on American soil; including a terrorist cell in Miami that was plotting an attack against the Sears Tower in Chicago, Illinois. One of the terrorists was quoted as stating *"They had hoped their attacks would be at least as good as or greater than the 9/11 attacks in New York City."* In another act of pre-planned violence, six men were arrested for plotting an attack at Fort Dix Army Base, and a third Al- Qaeda cell had planned a cyanide attack on a New York subway station that could have killed thousands.

The radical Islamic terrorists involved have been a part of our society; they work with us, live in our neighborhoods, and all the while are secretly planning on carrying out missions that would destroy America from within. Some have immigrated from foreign countries, but others are born and raised as US citizens. They are looking for spiritual fulfillment and a sense of belonging that they have not found elsewhere.

Islamic religious leaders are going into American prisons for the sole purpose of recruiting thousands of black males that feel as if they have been treated unfairly by our justice system; upon release back into society, these former inmates find local mosques and become adherents to Islam, those prone to violence are more drawn to the radical form of Islam.

The Islamic Movement in America uses deception as their primary tactic. Americans are being told that the mainstream Islamic groups are moderate; however, this is far from the truth. Groups such as CAIR (Council on American-Islamic Relations) present themselves as promoting peace and condemning violence, but when asked about specific terrorists groups such as Hamas or Hezbollah, they will not pointedly condemn them, while during their rallies they openly support them.

CAIR (Council on American Islamic Relations) is one of many Muslim interest groups that purport to represent the Islamic community in America, but in reality have well established ties to Hamas and other terror groups. Outside of its support for terror organizations, CAIR works to quickly and effectively to silence any discussions about radical Islam by playing the racism card and accusing critics of Islamophobia. CAIR's devices are effective.

Some of the most important leaders of the Islamic movement groups have an ulterior motive and use the groups as their smoke screen or cover for operations, such as Abdurahman Alamoudi, a Muslim leader for the American Muslim Council (AMC). He was videotaped speaking at rally sponsored by CAIR, and asks the question, "Is anybody a supporter of Hamas?" to which the crowd cries "Yes" in unison. He had direct connections to the White House during the Clinton and Bush administrations, and was photographed standing beside former President Bush smiling for the camera; he was viewed as a moderate Muslim. In 2004, he was arrested on terrorist charges for financing a terrorist campaign.

The FBI uncovered a 15 page secret document that is a Manifesto of the Muslim Brotherhood in America that outlines the goals and strategies in the US of

Islamists, note it is not radical Islamists, but mainstream Islam in America. On page 7, it refers to the "Grand Jihad", which entails eliminating and destroying western civilization from within, and to set up group mosques centers throughout America and declare "Allah" victorious over all other religions.

"The US needs to understand that the Jihadist machine is already in our society" -Dr. Walid Phares, Foundation for the Defense of Democracies

Melanie Phillips, author of *Londonistan*, stated, "America and Britain are in a state of denial as to what they are up against. Muslims do not accept settlements, as in *'When in Rome do as the Romans do'*. They do not accept British Law as it is, but want British law to accommodate Shari'ah Law for them."

The United Nations continues to pass one condemning judgment after another against Israel as illustrated in November 2012 at the United Nations General Assembly Meeting *[A/C.4/67/L.17]* in the supposed "occupation" of the Syrian Golan Heights, stating Israeli practices are affecting the human rights of the Palestinian people in occupied Palestinian territory including East Jerusalem. The Israelis had left the Golan Heights in 2005, and Hamas came to power there. This was subsequently followed by rockets launched into Israel from Hamas in the Golan Heights, so Israel is now blockading the Golan Heights to stop weapons smuggling from Egypt to supply Hamas. The UN seems to ignore the fact that the 'Golan Heights' acted aggressively after Israel evacuated the settlement; too many people support the Palestinian cause without understanding or caring about the true history of the region, or the true nature of the people that hate Israel without cause.

Demands that Israel, the occupying Power, cease all practices and actions that violate the human rights of the Palestinian people, including the killing and injury of civilians, the arbitrary detention and imprisonment of civilians and the destruction and confiscation of civilian property, and that it fully respect human rights law and comply with its legal obligations in this regard, including in accordance with relevant United Nations resolutions

Islam is a religion that does not adhere to the global definition of "human rights" when pressed upon by outsiders of their barbaric treatment of their own people by the practice of Shari'ah Law. Many Middle Eastern countries, such as Iran, refused to sign the *Universal Declaration for Human Rights* (UDHR) stating that it opposed the core of Islamic fundamentalism and Shari'ah Law.

In 1982, the Iranian representative to the United Nations, Said Rajaie-Khorassani, said that the UDHR was "a secular understanding of the Judeo-Christian tradition", which could not be implemented by Muslims without trespassing the Islamic law. On 30 June 2000, Muslim nations that are members of the Organization of the Islamic Conference (now the Organization of Islamic Cooperation) officially resolved to support the Cairo Declaration on Human Rights in Islam, an alternative document that says people have "freedom and right to a dignified life in accordance with the Islamic Shari'ah", without any discrimination on grounds of "race, color, language, sex, religious belief, political affiliation, social status or other considerations".

How can they disaffect the human rights of Palestinians who do not acknowledge the global definition of "human rights"? It is clear that the only time the Arabic Islamic countries are in favor of UN or US help is when their own laws do not support their cause. The basis for this constant struggle is the issue of whose land it really is, and that issue can only be proven on religious grounds. Islam was not formed as a religion until the seventh century AD, whereas Judaism has biblical and archaeological proof of existence as living in the land of Judea from the Babylonian conquest in the sixth century BC onwards; legally, the Arabs are occupying Israeli lands.

Amerislam?

The Branch Davidians, a religious cult compound in Waco, Texas, became entangled with law enforcement during the 1990's after drawing the attention of the FBI for stockpiling weapons which led to the death of 80 individuals, some women and children. The same development is occurring all across the US with hundreds of religious compounds springing up from coast to coast; the difference? The Davidians were a white American religious "cult", and the others are Islamic, one example of these compounds is actually called "Islamberg". This is not a defense of religious cults, however, constitutionally speaking, one has to wonder in a land of freedom, why a small group bearing arms and living together in a religious compound was targeted, yet we have compounds of Islamic Muslims living together financed by Arabic foreigners, bearing arms, practicing a religion that calls anyone outside of it an infidel. Does an American Christian present themselves with regards to their religion in the same manner as a Christian living in a foreign country? The answer is yes; however, the common rhetoric of Islam in Arabic countries is "America is the Enemy". In Iran, America is referred to as the "Great Satan" and Israel is only the "Little Satan".

Scary Statistics

According to Wikipedia:

In 2011 a Pew poll finds 1 out of every 10 Muslim Americans believe President Obama is really a Muslim.

91 percent of all honor-related killings around the world are carried out by Muslims (84% in US, 96% in Europe)

9 of the top 10 persecutors of Christians are Islamic countries. Of the top 50 countries, only 12 have a source other than Islam.

2012 report finds the majority of world's terrorism committed by Muslims. Almost 9000 deaths caused by Sunni terrorists in 2011.

Is America's head under the sand?

The leopard is the third out of four beasts. Next, we will dissect the last monster.

Leviathan

Leviathan the gliding serpent,

Leviathan the coiling serpent,

He will slay the monster of the sea.

— Isaiah 27:1

✚

Chapter 4

Part I

Heads of Leviathan

The abyssal zone, the scientific name is abyssopelagic, is located 13,000 feet below sea level. In its black and icy depths no ray of sunlight permeates the darkness. At 11,000 pounds of pressure, a human body will implode upon itself. The sea creatures that exist in this alien environment look like something from a science fiction movie; the known creatures that have been researched are either fanged or phosphorescent, some of them appear as tiny sea serpents such as the dragon fish and viper fish.

'The Abyss' is referred to throughout the bible, and especially in the book of Revelation, as water or a bottomless pit. The Greek word for abyss is "abussos", which means boundless or bottomless, an unfathomable depth; in Hebrew it is "tehom". Many scriptures refer to abyss as water *(Isaiah 63:12-13, Roman 10:7, Luke 8:31);* and Oxfords Bible describes abyss as 'depths of the sea'.

It is from this inhospitable and unfathomable environment, that John in Revelation and Daniel witness the rise of Leviathan.

After that, in my vision at night I looked and there before me was a fourth beast-terrifying and frightening and very powerful. It had large iron teeth: it crushed and devoured its victims and trampled underfoot whatever was left. It was different from all the former beasts, and it had ten horns. (Daniel 7:7)

Then I wanted to know the true meaning of the fourth beast, the one with iron teeth and bronze claws. (Daniel 7: 19)

And I saw a beast coming out of the sea. He had ten horns and seven heads, with ten crowns on his horns and on each head a blasphemous name. (Revelation 13:1-3)

This beast, like the others before it, is symbolic for an empire; an empire is a form of government that uses a system; the other beast empires included a monarchy, communism, and theocracy. This empire will not be like any other empire that we know of, but can speculate that it will be far more intense than the Nazi regime or the most radical form of Islam. This vision terrified Daniel, and he was living under a monarchy that had tried to take his life. The last beast will be the worst empire our world has ever seen; it will strip national sovereignty, and human rights from most countries on the planet. This beast empire will come into existence prior to the rise of the man we call the antichrist; he does not put this beast system together, only takes control of it during his rise to power, thereby forming a one world government. This beast is referred to elsewhere in the bible; consider the following verses:

²The beast I saw resembled a leopard, but had feet like those of a bear and a mouth like that of a lion. The dragon gave the beast his power and his throne and great authority.³One of the heads of the beast seemed to have had a fatal wound but the fatal wound had been healed. The whole world was astonished and followed the beast.
(Revelation 13:2-10)

Then the angel carried me away in the spirit into a desert. There I saw a woman sitting on a scarlet beast that was covered with blasphemous names and had seven heads and ten horns. (Revelation 17:3)

This calls for a mind with wisdom. The seven heads are seven hills on which the woman sits. They are also seven kings. Five have fallen, one is, the other has not yet come, but when he does come, he must remain for a little while. The beast who once was and now is not is an eighth king. He belongs to the seven and is going to his destruction. The ten horns you saw are ten kings who have not yet received a kingdom, but who for one hour will receive authority as kings along with the beast. They have one purpose and will give their power and authority to the beast. (Revelation 17:9-13)

The overall composite picture of the fourth beast is as follows:

Seven Heads-Seven World Empires that have already come as of World War II

Ten Horns –Ten Rulers that had not yet received a Kingdom as of 95 AD

Ten Crowns –On the heads of the ten rulers (horns) which denote authority

Body of a leopard-The Middle Eastern people of Islam

Iron Teeth-Roman form of government and execution

Bear feet-Russian Military Support

Bronze claws-Grasps the former Grecian territories of the Seleucid Dynasty

Blasphemous Names written on it (Calling itself God and wanting to be worshiped)

Mouth of a lion – Mouth of the Antichrist as a king that speaks boastfully

Eleventh horn that uprooted three other horns – This is the actual antichrist

The book of Revelation reveals more details as to the symbolism of the seven heads; they are explained as seven hills and also as seven kings. As explained previously in reference to the Islamic leopard, heads denote succession of rule. Most bible expositors agree the seven hills refer to Rome, and also because the woman that is sitting on them is the Vatican. The woman sitting on the hills, however, is much older than Rome itself. She is called "The Harlot" and "Mystery Babylon"; therefore the kings that she had control of extend much further back than Rome. The first king is referred to in Daniel, King Nebuchadnezzar...

The Seven Heads

First Head-Babylon

The mystery of the identity of the first "king" or "head" of the beast began in Babylon and ended up at Rome. The book of Daniel is the first time a 'seven' headed beast is mentioned in scripture, during which Daniel was exiled in Babylon and all of Daniel's prophecies point to the future. Many bible commentators feel that Egypt was the first head as the nation that kept Israel in bondage, but Israel had yet to be a nation when in bondage under pharaoh. Israel went into Egypt as a family of seventy people, and came out with more than a million, but still they had no homeland nor had they established themselves as a nation. Daniel was not the first time a "beast" with multiple heads was mentioned in scripture; Egypt was a blueprint of the future ransom of Israel from the fourth beast. Psalms 74:13-14 says *"It was you who broke the heads of the monster in the waters. It was you who crushed the heads of Leviathan."* The psalmist was obviously referring to the children of Israel being led through the Red Sea and Pharaoh was a type of symbolic "monster" being drowned in the waters. While doing research on Egyptian Pharaohs, it was noticed that although religious and academic scholars can't agree on exact dates of the Israelite captivity, they mostly do agree that the exodus took place during the eighteenth dynasty and feel that they went into Egypt sometime between the tenth to eleventh dynasty periods of time. That would have put the Israelites in captivity for the duration of seven dynasties, or seven heads on a beast, but that remains inconclusive unless a definite timeframe is set for the Israelites in Egypt; however, it explains the meaning for Psalm 74:13-14. Since the other heads of the beast had not become kingdoms when the exodus occurred, it could not have meant that God destroyed them at that time. Another argument that the heads do not include Egypt, is that it leaves no room for the rule of the Roman Catholic Church; the beast was responsible for 1200 years of tyranny, persecution, murder, and wars while the Roman Catholic Church was in power, and that is how the beast is last depicted in Revelation, with the Vatican astride it.

Many think that Egypt had to be the first head of the beast due to the timing of John writing Revelation, which was while Rome was in power. The phrase *"five have fallen, one is, and the other is still to come"* would seem that *"one is"* referred to Rome; thereby needing to look for two preceding kingdoms to Babylon which, they assume, would have been Egypt and Assyria. John, however, was in the spirit when he saw the harlot astride the beast in the desert. The phrase "in the desert" is indicative that she is not in power nor is the beast, and she was *"drunk with the blood of the saints"*, meaning after her reign. The entire scenario John portrays is of the Vatican between the time of 1798, when Napoleon put the pope under arrest, to immediately before the rise of Hitler to power and the commencement of World War II. John saw the beast with its last jockey, the Vatican, but before its final rider until the apocalypse, which was Adolf Hitler. Every word of scripture carries importance; while trying to decipher when John is viewing the beast, the phrase *"in the desert"* and *"drunk with the blood of saints"* is suggestive that the beast and harlot are in a "time out". The *"one is"* would have been the empire in power during the time frame of the 135 years of the beast in the desert, which was Great Britain, and the *"one that is to come for a short while"* would be the next

97

short lived empire after Great Britain, which was Adolf Hitler in Nazi Germany.

The final tip of the identity of the first head of the beast is the harlot herself; on her forehead was written, "Mystery Babylon" and she could not ride an animal until she came into existence. The Harlot could not have been Rome itself; as we discussed in the chapter one, that the kingdoms decreased in wealth after Babylon but the Harlot is portrayed as exceedingly wealthy. The golden cup in her hand is symbolic of the Catholic Mass service. Knowing which kingdom is the first head of the beast allows the reader to look for kingdoms that are subsequent to Babylon.

Second Head-Mede/Persian

The second head of the beast would have followed Babylon; it was the Mede/Persian Empire. At this point it should be noted that the last world empire will be a composite beast of world empires. As we saw, the beast has iron teeth (Rome) and Bronze Claws (Greece). Although the ancient world empires have passed away, the beast will use the greatest strengths of those empires to its advantage; for instance iron symbolizes the strength of the government and military in ancient Rome, and teeth are used to chew food. A picture of the cross should come to mind, as this was a form of execution invented by Rome. Claws symbolize how an animal grasps its prey and Bronze signifies divine judgment through the descendants of the Grecian Empire. Bronze claws represent a descendant of the former Seleucid territory of Greece, combined with the reign of the antichrist grasping its former territories in the Middle East; we will discuss this in detail further along.

Third Head-Greece

This head represents Greece under Alexander the Great and follows Mede/Persia. All of the empires that are symbolized by the heads of the monster were empires that affected the entire known world. The head representing Greece includes the four kingdoms that were depicted as four horns on the head of a shaggy goat that arose from his empire; Seleucid, Ptolemy, Lysimachus, and Cassander which were discussed in chapter 1. The rule of the Grecian Empire came to a close with the fall of the Seleucid Dynasty to Rome. Most of the Grecian territories came under the rule of the Turkish Empire after the fall of Rome in 476 AD, until Great Britain disbanded the Ottoman Empire in 1922 at the close of World War I. Greece had only recently gained its independence at the beginning of the nineteenth century with the help of Europe, and is now close to collapsing on itself economically, requiring the European Union to bail the country out from under staggering debt.

Fourth Head-Rome

The fourth head of the beast is Rome which ruled Judea from 63 BC until 476 AD after conquering the last Dynasty of Greece, the Seleucid Dynasty. There are two different forms of Rome; pagan Rome, which is this empire, and Papal Rome, which is the Roman Catholic Church under the administration of the papacy. After crucifying our Savior, pagan Rome destroyed the second temple in Jerusalem in 70 AD under the orders of Titus Flavius, and then the Emperor Hadrian ploughed over Jerusalem with a team of oxen in 135 AD. He also changed the name of the country from Judea to "Palestine" after the ancient

Jewish enemy, the Philistines, while trying to eradicate all memories of the Jewish people. The Jews were banned from entering Jerusalem on pain of death, and they remained exiled from their homeland for more than 1800 years; long after Rome ceased to exist as an empire. The Arabs migrated into the territory of Judea and the crusades were fought over the Holy Land, but the Arabs never rebuilt Jerusalem other than the Dome of the Rock, which was built on the temple mount. Early Christian travelers to the Holy Land reported that it was a wasteland, that one could travel over the entire region and not see a single soul. The UN has not properly researched history when asking the Jewish people to return portions of her land, nor do they adhere to the Balfour Declaration, whereby the entire land of Judea including Jordan was originally given to the Jewish people in 1917. The territory was called Palestine until the Jewish people renamed it "Israel" in 1945. It is ironic to hear Arabs calling this land "Palestine" as if it were an Arabian name, when the name "Palestine" was given to it by a Roman Emperor two thousand years ago, to vex the Jewish people. The fact that, in Roman history, the Emperor Hadrian went to such great lengths to eradicate Jewish customs, such as circumcision which was only practiced by Jews, in the land that is now Israel only strengthens the case that the land has belonged to the Jews for over two millennia. The world tries to erase biblical history, and even Jewish history, however; they cannot erase all history, of which Rome has given its testimony.

Fifth Head-Papal Rome and the Holy Roman Empire

The Holy Roman Empire was the First Reich of Germany. The Roman Imperial Title was first granted to Charlemagne when he was crowned King of the Franks on Christmas Day in 800 AD by Pope Leo III. The Roman Catholic Church should have abstained from involving itself in political affairs; the scriptures are clear in that Christians, and especially the clergy, should be interested in the affairs of the kingdom of God, not of men.

(2 Timothy 2:4) "No one serving as a soldier gets involved in civilian affairs. He wants to please his commanding officer." Because of this involvement, God considered the Roman Catholic Church a "Harlot"; his supposed 'bride' is chasing after kings and crowns.

Under Charlemagne, France and Germany was a combined kingdom; the Emperor became known as the "Father of Europe" as his empire united most of Western Europe for the first time since the Roman Empire fell. Today the modern countries that comprised the Holy Roman Empire included Germany, Austria, Belgium, Czech Republic, Liechtenstein, Luxembourg, Monaco, The Netherlands, San Marino, Slovenia, Switzerland, France, Italy, and Poland.

The Roman Catholic Church had gained momentous power in the 324 years since the fall of Rome itself; it was sometime during those years that the Church of Rome had begun its move away from the image of Christ to an institution of ill repute. With the church's involvement in political affairs, it was a precedent set for the proceeding popes to follow; in general, to do anything they chose without moral conscience or biblical guidelines. The very worst popes followed in the footsteps of Pope Leo III, dragging the church in a downward spiral into an abyss of chaos, murder, torture, debauchery and scandal. It was the power of the entwinement of church and state that allowed 1200 years of suffocating dominion by the Vatican; laymen were not even allowed to have their own bible;

the church was the only authority that claimed could interpret scripture. The harlot riding the beast became one with the empire she controlled. This head of the beast survived a millennium, longer than any other head would rule; thereby creating the worst and darkest chapter in human history to date.

After the 'Great Schism' in 1095; the weaker Constantinople (modern Istanbul in Turkey), lost its power struggle to keep up with Rome. Most of the earliest churches founded in Asia Minor began to gradually revert to Islam. Television documentaries depicting the sites of the earliest churches of Asia Minor that were established by Paul show they are nothing more than historical ruins now. After a thousand years of struggle and persecution, the once Christian "eastern leg" of Rome became pagan again in the form of the new religion of Islam. That is of importance, considering that the body of the beast is people of Middle Eastern origin; for those people comprised the right leg of Rome.

It was following the schism in 1198 that Rome, under papal approval, began the first of the three crusades followed by the Inquisition. Revelation goes into great detail about the cargoes purchased by the Vatican, the end of the verse is: *(Revelation 18:13)"and the bodies and souls of men"*. The practice of selling indulgences by the Catholic Church was no secret; the concept of purgatory is unscriptural, and to ask a parishioner to pay a price for a priest to release a loved one's soul from purgatory is not only pagan, but predatory as well. The army of the crusades consisted of average men that the pope had promised to completely absolve them of all sin if they would take up the sword in the name of Christ. It is contrary to scripture, consider the following verses: *(Mathew 26: 51-52) One of Jesus' companions reached for his sword and struck the servant of the high priest, cutting off his ear. "Put your sword back in its place for all who draw the sword will die by the sword." Jesus said to him.*

The Roman Catholic Church had completely taken on another identity; instead of the image of Christ, one of a harlot. God levels these charges among many others at her and tells his people to *"come out of her so that you will not share in her sins or receive any of her plagues, for her sins are piled up to heaven and God has remembered her crimes" (Revelation 18: 4-5)* Taking part in the practices of the Roman Catholic faith is equivalent to harboring a fugitive, and by continuing to be a parishioner of a church that has many pagan practices, and is considered a criminal, is being defiant to God. He extolls "His people" to come out of her.

The Roman Catholic Church outlived the empire she created and the kings she controlled. She is still very much alive, and has parishioners across the globe. Her end is coming; *"In her heart she boasts, 'I sit as queen; I am not a widow, and I will never mourn'. Therefore in one day her plagues will overtake her: death, mourning and famine. She will be consumed by fire, for mighty is the Lord God who judges her. (Revelation 18:7-8)*

Sixth Head - Great Britain

This head physically came into being in 1534 when Henry VIII divorced England from Papal Rome by setting up "The Act of Supremacy", thereby making Henry VIII the 'Head of the Church of England'. This led to the Reformation of England under protestant leaders; the dissolution of the monasteries in England helped Henry finance his fortifications in the Navy, making future maritime exploration possible. It was not until Henry's daughter Elizabeth I took the throne that England was completely reformed and protestant. Her 45 years of English rule provided economic and religious stability to England, and a chance for further explorations in new lands. By 1606 the first colony at Jamestown, and one of the oldest of England's colonies, had been established by the Scottish King James I after two previously unsuccessful attempts under Queen Elizabeth; as well as their already established colonies in India as the East India Company. The biggest export of the 13 original colonies in America was the tobacco crop, however, the colonies were exploited through cheap tobacco prices by the English crown, and plantation owners found themselves deeply in debt to the English before the Revolutionary War. England lost their hold on America after the War of Independence, but they still retained the largest empire in the history of the world. They colonized wherever they explored and their empire grew; at the peak of their empire, Great Britain had colonies spanning the globe, from the Americas, to the African subcontinent, to Hong Kong and all areas in between.

World War I brought a substantial financial strain on Great Britain, which relied heavily on its colonies. At the end of World War I, Great Britain began dismantling its colonies in the Middle East. The British relinquished control of Palestine following the Holocaust to the Jewish people at the end of World War II, which finally gave the Jews a homeland for the first time in 1878 years. Britain is no longer an empire; it has come full circle, now finding itself in almost the exact situation as was left by Henry VIII. The power in Europe has been equalized by the European Union, and seems to be on track to becoming the "One World Government" described by the apostle John in Revelation. This brings us to the final "head" of the beast.

Seventh Head-The Fuhrer & Nazi Germany

Five have fallen, one is, and the other has not yet come, but when he does come, he must remain a short while. (Revelation 17:10).

The years of 1933 to 1945 have not been easily forgotten by the generation that lived through them, and especially in Europe. After the stock market crashed, the world was hurled into the Great Depression followed on the heels by World War II. The world had already been torn apart by World War I combined with an outbreak of deadly flu that killed millions across the globe. It left a vacuum effect in countries such as Germany, which had been in decline with high unemployment rates since the late nineteenth century. The combination of all these factors left Germany in need of a 'savior' to take control of the country; Adolf Hitler was the answer. He became a member of the National Socialist German Workers Party in 1921 after his service during World War I; and attempted a coup d'état in 1923 in Munich which failed, landing Hitler in prison. Anti-Semitism was a popular sentiment in Austria and Germany before Hitler was appointed to office. It was during his imprisonment that he wrote 'Mein Kampf' (My Struggle); he also became obsessed with the concept of a pure Aryan race of blond haired blue eyed peoples, but he himself appeared to have roots of a far different nationality. An excerpt from an online article in the *dailymail* states:

"One author who has researched the family tree is German author Ralf Jahn who claims mental illness was rife among the Hitler tribe. The Führer was terrified when he lived that this dark secret would emerge and went to great lengths to keep it hidden. His cousin was exterminated in a death camp because she suffered from schizophrenia.

He carried the concept of a 'pure Aryan race' into office when he was appointed the Chancellor of Germany on January 30, 1933. He took the reins of Germany during the midst of the Great Depression, when the rest of the world was struggling and unemployment rates were skyrocketing in other European countries. During the first year of his chancellorship, the Nazi Party set in motion 'The Enabling Act' which allowed Hitler to eliminate all opposition and set up the Gestapo; so that by 1934, he had become the sole leader of Germany, which unofficially changed his status from "Chancellor" to "Dictator". Under the ideals of Nazism, Germany became an autocratic totalarian government. The Fuhrer and the Nazi Party restored economic stability in Germany during his first year in office which silenced criticism from the general public. He gave the German people a sense of pride and nationalism that had been dwindling into nonexistence in previous years.

The hypnotic effects of his charismatic oratory lulled and captivated his audiences. The German people were brainwashed with the "Nazi Propaganda" being thrown at them by his public relations department. During the Third Reich, women's rights were curtailed, enrollment in educational studies by women plummeted as it was referred to as a by-product of Jewish education. Hitler stressed women should stay home and procreate to populate the Aryan race; taking care of their families should be their sole priority. The Hitler 'Youth Program' insured early indoctrination of Nazi Ideology. Hitler not only wanted to control the government of Germany, but he also wanted to control the individual by using brainwashing and mind control techniques through his propaganda program. These same principles are in use under Shari'ah Law within Islam, and are especially prevalent in the Middle Eastern countries where the majority of the population is Islamic.

'The only religion I respect is Islam. The only prophet I admire is the Prophet Muhammad.' -- Adolf Hitler (from "The Mysterious Achmed Huber: Friend to Hitler")

Although it is an under-researched topic with much sensationalism, there is little doubt that Hitler was also obsessed with the occult and immersed in occultic practices; his obsession with the 'Spear of Destiny', the 'Holy Grail', and other religious relics led the Nazi Party in search of these artifacts. Sources closest to him reported that he was known to spend hours walking in the garden where he appeared to be having a conversation with someone, yet he was alone. The majority of the population believes the sensational connection of Hitler to the occult because of his barbaric actions, and his mesmerizing spell he seemed to cast on his audiences. Everyone knew there was something "amiss" in Adolf Hitler, something more than an evil regime; yet it remained an intangible element that was occurring in Germany during the years of 1933 to 1945.

The reason behind the occult lore and Hitler is that of a 1,900 year old prophecy written by John in Revelation while exiled on the isle of Patmos awaiting Roman execution. Adolf Hitler was born for his destiny to be the seventh head of the world empire beast, to initiate the astounding destruction that ultimately led to his attempt in annihilating the Jewish people of Europe. He was propelled by a power that was not his own; Satan has always hated the Jewish people, and this was another attempt to destroy them. It is not sensational, but prophetic; the world looks in shadowy corners of the occult for a reasonable explanation behind the actions of a madman. Hitler was under demonic and satanic influence, of that there is no room for doubt in the Christian realm. The majority of Christians today are unaware of the significance of Hitler's role in the seventh head of the beast, and the frightening part is that it is to be repeated on a much larger scale in the future. Like the Vatican, Hitler was one with the beast also. He felt that it was his destiny to rule Germany, and he erringly thought he was appointed by God; yet he held no high regard for Christians, and would speak disparagingly of Christianity, calling it "weak".

When reading through the complicated verses of Revelation in relation to the beast, the angel tells John two things: the heads of the beast are in power, yet the actions or "body" of the beast can be dormant.

"The Body" -The inhabitants of the earth will be astonished when they see the beast because he once was, <u>now is not</u> and yet will come. The beast who once was, and now is not is an eighth king; he belongs to the seven and is going to his destruction. (Revelation 17:8-11)

"The Heads"-Five have fallen, one is, and the other has not yet come. (Revelation 17: 9)

The angel tells John the "beast" is not in power when he saw him in the desert, yet the head is active (this would have been the head of the British Empire); meaning that the head in power controls the body, and a docile head would control a docile body, such as Great Britain.

It also tells us **"the inhabitants of the earth will be astonished when they see the beast because he once was, now is not and yet will come".** Various other words with the same meaning of "astonished" are surprised, amazed, speechless, and shocked; the question is why? Scripture states **"because he once was"**; of all the heads of the beast that existed, the only one that would shock this generation to see, and the only one that would even be recognizable in the present age would be Hitler. No other empire was so closely connected to its leader as was Nazi Germany, as Hitler was the only leader of the Nazi regime before it ceased to exist. The other world empires continued to operate through the revolutions of many leaders over the course of many years. The Vatican still has an office, yet it no longer has a beast; in Revelation 17:16 scriptures tell us that:

"The beast and the ten horns will hate the prostitute (meaning the Vatican), they will bring her to ruin and leave her naked."

This statement eliminates the Vatican and the Papacy from ever coming to power again with the beast; I know that statement is a serious disappointment for those who believe the antichrist will be the Vatican and a future pope. The "antichrist" will be foes with the Christian religion from the beginning as we will discuss later on.

Estimates of mortality rates by direct or indirect methods (the inquisition and the crusades from soldiers to civilians) under direction of the popes is anywhere from several hundred thousand to several million depending on the party supplying the information. Even should the estimate reach over one million, it was amassed within a space of 1,200 years of power; compare to Hitler's Jewish solution culminating in the death of 6 million Jews, and approximately a total of 20 million people altogether in a mere 12 years.

One of the heads of the beast seemed to have had a fatal wound, but the fatal wound had been healed. The whole world was astonished and followed the beast. (Revelation 13:3)

When the allied troops took Berlin, Hitler knew he had lost not only the war but control of his country as well. In April of 1945 in a bunker under the 'Wolf's Lair' he committed suicide by biting down on a cyanide capsule and simultaneously putting a gun to his head and pulling the trigger.

He died from a "fatal head wound", and Nazi Germany died with him. He is the only leader in the only empire to expire in this fashion; *of a fatal head wound.* He was the seventh head of the beast, therefore, the seventh head of the beast died from a fatal head wound. (Revelation 13:14) *"He ordered them to set up an image in honor of the beast who was wounded by the sword and yet lived".* The word "sword" means war, during wartime, or because of war. Hitler committed suicide during wartime to escape capture by the Russian Army. The fact that John sees the beast come up out of the sea with a fatal head wound means that one of the original seven heads was wounded; so this eliminates a future eighth king from being hurt and revived. This has already happened historically. To understand which head or empire is the returning eighth king, one can search history for the wounded head. In scriptures, some prophecies are allegorical and some are actual events; in example, the beast itself is allegorical, symbolic of many empires, while the head wound is an actual death sentence of the leader and empire associated with that head.

The whole world was astonished because they witness a man returning from the dead. Whether or not he is exactly the same, the antichrist will have Hitler's oratory skill and personality and more than likely look like him as well. He will be the eighth king, but he will not surface in Germany again as we will discuss in the chapter, "The Eighth King".

He once was, now is not, and yet will come. He will come up out of the Abyss and go to his destruction. (Revelation 17:8)

John saw the beast in the desert after the destruction the Papacy caused during her rule; yet the angel tells John that the beast will only come once more. The only possibility that remains is the seventh and eighth heads are the same. Verse eight states "he once was" (The Roman Catholic Church), "now is not" (British Empire) "yet he will come" (under Hitler in 1933) and again "he will come up out of the Abyss and go to his destruction" (during the reign of the eighth king). The beast must first go into the Abyss before he can come up out of it; the last location of the beast is in the desert with the harlot. From the "desert" he goes to Germany; and following Hitler's suicide, to the watery Abyss, where he waits for his last chance under the

111

control of the eighth king which is none other than Hitler re-embodied. There are many that would disagree with a "re-appearance" of Hitler; however, the bible specifically states that the eighth king returns from the dead, and that he is of the 'seven'. It is the reason the population at large is astonished when they realize who he is.

The abyss is a jail cell for demons:

Jesus asked him "What is your name?" "Legion" he replied, because many demons had gone into him. And they begged him repeatedly not to order them to go into the Abyss. (Luke 8:31)

The fifth angel sounded his trumpet, and I saw a star that had fallen from the sky to the earth. The star was given the key to the shaft of the Abyss. (Revelation 9:1)

The beast and rider have been entombed in the Abyss since 1945; the only time the beast has actually perished was during Hitler's control. When sent into the desert with the harlot, it was because the Vatican lost its grip on the power she wielded; whatever the fate of the rider, becomes the fate of the beast also. The desert is an 'arid' place where demons go when evicted or exorcised from a human; isolation or a "time out".

When an evil spirit comes out of a man, it goes through <u>arid places</u> seeking rest and does not find it. (Mathew 12:43)

The Beast is incarcerated; waiting for its return as the eighth and final kingdom:

The beast who once was, and now is not, is an eighth king. <u>He belongs to the seven</u> and is going to his destruction. (Revelation 17:11)

To recap, the seven heads in chronological order were:

> Babylon
> Mede/Persia
> The Empire of Greece
> The Roman Empire
> Papal Rome and the Holy Roman Empire
> The British Empire
> The Third Reich

Now that we have identified the "Heads" of the beast, we will examine the "Body".

Part II
Ten Horns & Ten Crowns

It was different from all the former beasts, and it had ten horns. (Daniel 7:7)

And I saw a beast coming out of the sea. He had ten horns and seven heads, with ten crowns on his horns. (Revelation 13:1)

The ten horns you saw are ten kings who have not yet received a kingdom, but who for one hour will receive authority (crowns) as kings along with the beast. They have one purpose and will give their power and authority to the beast. (Revelation 17:12-13)

The legacy of Rome is still alive and well all around us; it exists in our city water pipes, in our sewage and waste systems, in our government and military, and in our civil engineering. Rome was the legs of iron on a statue connected to the feet and toes of brittle clay and iron. As discussed previously, Rome was a divided kingdom physically between East and West, and spiritually between church and state. The proportions of the body of the metal statue in Daniel are accurate with regard to the two legs being a divided kingdom having two capitals (Rome and Constantinople); therefore the "ten" toes are also significant. There are verses that allude to the ten toes:

While you were watching a rock was cut out, but not by human hands. It struck the statue on its feet of iron and clay and smashed them. Then the iron, the clay, the bronze, the silver, and the gold were broken to pieces at the same time and became like chaff on a threshing floor in the summer. The wind swept them away without leaving a trace. But the rock that struck the statue became a huge mountain and filled the whole earth. (Daniel 2:34-35)

For to us a child is born, to us a son is given, and the government will be on his shoulders, and he will be called Wonderful Counselor, Mighty God, Everlasting Father, Prince of Peace. Of the increase of his government and peace there will be no end, he will reign on David's throne and over his kingdom, establishing and upholding it with justice and righteousness from that time on and forever. (Isaiah 9:6)

The above verses go together and the latter explains the former. When Christ returns to set up his kingdom, the previous kingdoms of the world will be destroyed along with the "clay" or mankind's version of "worship"; but his kingdom (huge mountain) will cover the entire earth, there will be no competition. He will have expectations for every person in every land during his millennial reign, and the nations that do not comply will not receive rain.

Then all the survivors from all the nations that have attacked Jerusalem will go up year after year to worship the King, the Lord Almighty, and to celebrate the feast of Tabernacles. If any of the peoples of the earth do not go up to Jerusalem to worship the King, the Lord Almighty, they will have no rain. (Zechariah 14:16-17)

Since the verses in Daniel of Christ's millennial reign have not come to pass yet, the toes are yet to have "substance"; they are not readily identifiable to the world. As the toes are connected to the feet, and the feet were a divided kingdom of Rome and Constantinople with formation of the Roman Catholic Church, then the toes will exist in the same location as the territories of ancient Rome. As the feet are divided, so are the toes, five toes on the European continent and five toes in the Middle Eastern Region. Since Rome is considered west, then all countries "west" of Rome (Rome included) are European, and Constantinople (Istanbul), located in modern Turkey is east then anything from the east of Rome to the Middle East that ancient Rome controlled would be "east" including Greece, but limited to the ancient boundaries of the furthest eastern Mede/Persian empire or present day Iran/Iraq. Some prophecy commentators think that these ten regions or countries will be formed by the antichrist or the beast system, however, they possibly already exist today as modern countries. When John wrote Revelation, in 95 AD, he was told that the ten crowns on the ten horns were rulers who had not yet received a kingdom; however, it does not mean that the countries, or kingdoms, themselves haven't been established since that time. The use of the word "crowns" indicates that they receive authority as kings during the reign of the last beast. The beast is the governmental system, the horns are the kings or rulers of territories controlled under that system and the crowns indicate they have authority. Immediately following this description, it states that they give their authority to the beast for "one hour", and they wage war against Jesus when he returns. Therefore the kings cannot receive their kingdoms until during the reign of the eighth king as they must be alive at the time that Christ returns.

There is a difference of significance between what Daniel saw, and what John saw in Revelation; it is the same beast, however, Daniel saw the beast before the

116

ten horns received their crowns; John saw the beast after the horns were crowned. The horns have one purpose, and that is to give their power and authority to the beast system. The reason John saw the beast with the crowns was because he was alive during the time of Roman Rule which is where the ten toes stem from, whereas Daniel saw it some 500 years earlier. They were crowned during John's vision which means the ten countries or regions stem from the provinces of ancient Rome; ancient Rome controlled territory from Britain to Egypt to Iraq, it was a huge empire. The five western toes can be any combination of the countries in modern Europe; the five toes of the eastern region are a smaller geographical area, but most of the Middle East has been newly annexed in the twentieth century, thereby giving old kingdoms a new government and boundaries.

The other factor is that not only is the toes made of iron, but clay as well. Clay signifies "religion" or "worship" by a human being made of the earth or clay; we are referred to as clay in the potter's hands. By acknowledging we are the clay, we are acknowledging God as our creator. In some biblical translations, it is referred to "miry" clay, meaning soft or wet which could be interpreted as "unbaked". This could be in reference to the condition of mankind during the end times. It is notated throughout scripture that clay, dust, refers to man and his relationship to God.

The Lord God formed the man from the dust of the ground and breathed into his nostrils the breath of life and the man became a living being. (Genesis 2:7)

By the sweat of your brow you will eat your food until you return to the ground, since from it you were taken; for dust you are and to dust you will return. (Genesis 3:19)

"You turn things upside down, as if the potter were thought to be like the clay! Shall what is formed say to him who formed it, "He did not make me"? Can the pot say of the potter "He knows nothing"? (Isaiah 29:16)

We are aware of two facts at this point, the first is that the antichrist will hate the Roman Catholic Church; and second, the body of the beast is a leopard which is the Middle Eastern people who adhere to Islam. We know the toes are a mixture of Iron and Clay, Iron being the government portion and clay the religious aspect; but in this modern era the right leg of ancient Rome, which was "Christian Catholic" Constantinople in Turkey, is now an almost totally Muslim community. We can therefore draw the conclusion from these facts that the religious portion, which was once the Roman Catholic Church, will be replaced by Islam in the finality of five of the ten toes which becomes the ten horns of the beast.

And he was given authority over every tribe, people, language and nation. (Revelation 13:7)

Though the beast will mainly dominate Europe and especially the Middle East, every country on the planet will be affected by the "One World Government".

Part III
Iron Teeth in a Lion's Mouth

The beast was given a mouth to utter proud words and blasphemies and to exercise his authority for forty-two months. He opened his mouth to blaspheme God, and to slander his name and his dwelling place and those who live in heaven. (Revelation 13:5-6)

The beast I saw resembled a leopard, but had feet like those of a bear and mouth like that of a lion. (Revelation 13:2)

In my vision at night I looked, and there before me was a fourth beast-terrifying and frightening and very powerful. It had large iron teeth; it crushed and devoured its victims and trampled underfoot whatever was left. (Daniel 7:7)

The Roman Empire has been referred to as a marvel in its engineering feats and its machine like efficiency. It was considered a bright and shining light that, after its fall, plunged the European continent into an engulfing darkness which lasted a thousand years; awaiting the birth of the Renaissance and Age of Enlightenment. The truth of the Roman Empire was revealed in its barbarity. Not only did the Romans invent crucifixion as a death penalty, but many other increasingly heinous forms of execution were put on display for the general public. A man suspended in midair with only nails in his wrists and ankles to support his body weight would have been agony, however, the public became bored with such mundane executions. Coliseums were built, not only for the games of the Gladiators, but to make sport of those condemned to the death penalty. It was not only the Roman government itself that was bloodthirsty, but the entire populace of Rome. The crowds would cheer and jeer as the prisoners were thrown into the arena to await whatever the 'Master of the Games' decided would be the entertainment of the day. In as much as the peoples of Rome were cultured, they were twice as barbaric. It has been quoted that "A society is measured by how it treats its weakest members" by several different people including Winston Churchill. Rome was measured and found lacking in civility and mercy.

The iron teeth of Rome will again chew and devour its victims when in the mouth of the last beast empire. Those who would oppose the "New World Government" system will be systematically deposed. The Christians living during this time period will again, as in ancient Rome during the early church, not only be persecuted but executed as well. The favored form of punishment of this beast system would appear to be decapitation as referred to in scriptures:

I saw thrones on which were seated those who had been given authority to judge. And I saw the souls of those who had been beheaded because of their testimony for Jesus and because of the word of God. They had not worshiped the beast or his image and had not received his mark on their foreheads or their hands. (Revelation 20:4)

Interestingly, the preferred form of execution in the current Middle Eastern countries of Saudi Arabia, Qatar, Yemen, and Iran is beheading; Saudi Arabia (the original birthplace of Islam) being the most frequent user of this form of execution. In 2012,

Amnesty International said it had recorded at least 79 executions in the country, 27 of them were foreigners.

Death by beheading is not such a thing of the past in Europe, the last head in France was removed in 1977 by the guillotine. Victor Hugo was quoted as saying "One can have a certain indifference to the death penalty as long as one has not seen a guillotine with one's own eyes".

The mindset of the people of Germany during Hitler's rule was either to ignore the plight of the Jews, show indifference, or voluntarily hand over the Jews to the Gestapo. In the Roman Empire the crowds applauded and enjoyed the violence. Scriptures tell us how the people living at the time this last beast comes to power will react to the plight of Christians; God will send two witnesses to preach during the last 42 months of the beast's rule. These two witnesses will prophesy for 1260 days, and then they are slain.

Their bodies will lie in the street of the great city, which is figuratively called Sodom and Egypt, where also their Lord was crucified. For three and a half days men from every people, tribe, language and nation will gaze on their bodies and refuse them burial. The inhabitants of the earth will gloat over them and will celebrate by sending each other gifts, because these two prophets had tormented those who live on the earth. (Revelation 11:8-10)

This next verse describes everyday life in our time, yet it is described as "terrible times in the last days":

But mark this: There will be terrible times in the last days. People will be lovers of themselves, lovers of money, boastful, proud, abusive, disobedient to their parents, ungrateful, unholy, without love, unforgiving, slanderous, without self-control, brutal, not

lovers of the good, treacherous, rash, conceited, lovers of pleasure
rather than lovers of God... Having a form of Godliness but
denying its power. Have nothing to do with them. (2 Timothy 3:2)

Few countries in the world now have a monarchy as a government. Great Britain was referred to as a "Lion Beast", and lions are associated with kingship as far back as King Solomon in the Old Testament.

Then the king made a great throne inlaid with ivory and overlaid
with fine gold. The throne had six steps, and it back had a rounded
top. On both sides of the seat were armrests, with a lion standing
beside each of them. Twelve lions stood on the six steps, one at
either end of each step. (1 Kings 10:18)

Jesus, the King of Kings and Lord of Lords, is called the Lion of the tribe of Judah.

Then one of the elders said to me, "Do not weep! See, the Lion of
the tribe of Judah, the Root of David, had triumphed. He is able to
open the scroll and its seven seals" (Revelation 5:5)

We have established that lions are associated with kings and monarchies; therefore the phrase "mouth of a lion" implies that the antichrist is speaking as a king or monarch. Though he will rule over European countries, he is not from Great Britain; his origins will be discussed in the next chapter. The mouth of a lion simply implies that he has ultimate authority, and it could also imply that he took the monarchy of Great Britain away from it for himself, since the United Kingdom will more than likely be a part of his dominion. **"The other beasts had been stripped of their authority, but were allowed to live for a period of time." (Daniel 7:12)** Kings speak boastfully, they have no master, they rule their own empire; a king fears nothing; a wise king would fear God. The antichrist is depicted as "the eighth king". The antichrist, under the power of Satan, literally hates God, his creator. He is so prideful and arrogant that he **"blasphemes God, slanders his name and his dwelling place and those who live there." (Revelation 13:6)** This is the reason he **"makes war with the saints" (Revelation 13:7)**; because of the animosity he feels towards God Almighty.

Until the eighth king comes to power, the beast has never truly had a voice, has never been able to "give its opinion". Though Hitler did not speak highly of Christianity, neither did he slander God, at least in public. The Roman Catholic Church was of Christian origin, and has always been under the impression that they are serving God. The seven headed beast is none other than Satan the dragon, the great serpent cast out of heaven, and he was prideful enough to argue with God and war with God's angels.

Then another sign appeared in heaven, an enormous red dragon with seven heads and ten horns and seven crowns on his heads. (Revelation 12:3)

Here we see the true beast, Satan. The reason there are only seven crowns depicted in this verse, is found in Daniel:

While I was thinking about the horns, there before me was another horn, a little one, which came up among them; and three of the first horns were uprooted before it. This horn had eyes like the eyes of a man, and a mouth that spoke boastfully. (Daniel 7:8)

The first three "horns" or regions (countries) will be replaced by the antichrist. The number seven has meaning in scripture, God created the heavens and earth in six days and on the seventh he rested; seven is the number of finality or completion. The earth has 7,000 years under the dominion of man, and there are seven world empires, it is a number that is repeated throughout scriptures such as the Temple of Solomon was completed in seven years. The Jews were given 'seventy' 'sevens' or 'weeks of years'; there is a final 'week' to come consisting of seven years. The book of Revelation has the final plagues and wrath of God as seven vials, bowl judgments, and seals; they are announced by seven angels blowing seven trumpets; there are seven thunders that speak, and seven churches. The number seven is connected to divine intervention from heaven or occurring in the spiritual realm that we cannot "see" but feel the effects of. It will be the finality of the world as we know it, the world Christ returns to will be in shambles; most of the world's population will be gone:

I will make man scarcer than pure gold, rarer than the gold of Ophir. (Isaiah 13:12)

Therefore a curse consumes the earth; its people must bear their guilt. Therefore earth's inhabitants are burned up, and very few are left (Isaiah 24:6)

The earth itself will endure cataclysmic events that it never recovers from, most of the earth as we know it will not support life again as it will be destroyed:

See, the lord is going to lay waste the earth and devastate it; he will ruin its face and scatter its inhabitants. (Isaiah 24:1)

The earth dries up and withers, the world languishes and withers, the exalted of the earth languish. (Isaiah 24:4)

The floodgates of the heavens are opened; the foundations of the earth shake. The earth is broken up, the earth is split asunder, the earth is thoroughly shaken. The earth reels like a drunkard, it sways like a hut in the wind, so heavy upon it is the guilt of its rebellion that it falls —never to rise again. (Isaiah 24:18-20)

In that day, the Lord will punish with his sword, his fierce, great and powerful sword, Leviathan the gliding serpent, Leviathan the coiling serpent; he will slay the monster of the sea. (Isaiah 27:1)

The cities of the earth will not be rehabilitated; the Lord will rule over this broken planet and what is left of the population because he is the final king on planet earth, and he will reign for a millennium, and then the old heavens and earth will pass away.

Then I saw a new heaven and a new earth for the first heaven and the first earth had passed away, and there was no longer any sea. (Revelation 21:1)

Part IV
Bear Feet and Bronze Claws

Russia has been dormant for twenty-two years, since the collapse of the Soviet Union in 1991. Like a bear, Russia is hibernating; it has needed time to repair itself internally. Had it not been for the Red Army of Russian troops during World War II, Hitler and Mussolini would not have been defeated so quickly. The wolf thought he could take the bears' cave away from him, but Germany was poorly prepared to face a Russian winter. The people of Russia survive some of the harshest winter climates on earth, which gave its army an advantage of endurance. They also have a strong sense of national pride; Russians love Russia, and are willing to fight to preserve their country, unlike the French that did not even put up a resistance to the Nazis. We have seen the military capability of Russia in the past, the phrase "get up and eat your fill of flesh" is the motto of the bear. The collapse of the Soviet Union meant to Russia, "Give us a few decades; we'll be on our feet again".

They have gone through many cycles of dormancy and aggression, from the Czars to the current Russian President Vladimir Putin. President Putin was a former cold war KGB agent, and in recent years has taken a more aggressive stance than his predecessor. With the current civil war in Syria, Russia held their position of allies for two years with the current Syrian Ba'ath party, until they found themselves alone on that position. There is a prophetic as well as a strategic reason as to why Russia continued to support a leader of a country that has violated the human rights and boundaries set by the Geneva Convention for countries incurring a civil war. The strategic reason being Syria is Russia's Middle Eastern ally, and has given Russia a naval base in the Mediterranean. The prophetic reason is found in the books of Daniel and Revelation:

Then I wanted to know the true meaning of the fourth beast, which was different from all the others and most terrifying, with its iron teeth and bronze claws. (Daniel 8:19)

The beast I saw resembled a leopard but had feet like those of a bear. (Revelation 13:2)

This beast is symbolic of an animal, and the claws of an animal are attached to its feet. The kingdom of Greece was of bronze, and the four dynasties that emerged from Alexander's original kingdom were also bronze, including the Seleucid Dynasty. The Seleucid Kings ruled from their base in ancient Syria; therefore Syria is still a bronze kingdom. Syria, along with all the other countries that were a part of the Seleucid kingdom, is the "bronze claws" of the last world empire beast. The claws are not independent of the feet of the animal, which are a "bear's feet", and feet allow the animal movement. The movement of a country is by its military, as a country itself doesn't move. The Russians have supported Syria because the two will be connected during the last world empire. Syria is a major arms purchaser from Russia and Russian banks are holding more than $6 billion in Syrian Assets.

Russia also supports Iran's Nuclear Programs against the position of US and Israel. In 2009, the inauguration of the nuclear facility known as Bushehr on the Persian Gulf from Russia to Iran expanded Russian/Iranian Nuclear Cooperation; (OPK), the Old Russian Defense Industrial Complex continues to promote the traditional strategic and economic ties with China, India, Iran, Syria, and North Korea.

The Russian military will play a large role in military operations carried out under the orders of the antichrist. Russia is currently a major supplier of arms and nuclear technologies to Arab nations; the latest, a bidding war between the Saudis and Iran over ground to air missiles. Russia's support lies within the body of the leopard more so than with the West or other European countries. It considers itself an equal partner to the European Union, with the EU being the largest trading partner to Russia; however, militarily it aligns itself towards the Middle East.

Russia is still in its cave, but is no longer asleep. According to a recent article in the Washington Times, Vladimir Putin has called for a massive Russian Military upgrade by 2016, after the US and Israel successfully tested a new missile defense system called "Arrow 3", which is used for shooting down long range missiles. A report by SIPRI (Stockholm International Peace Research Institute), from a Reuter's article, stated Russia spent nearly $72 billion on arms in 2011 and is planning further increases with draft budgets showing a 53% rise in real terms up to 2014. It also stated that Russia and China recently voiced unity in opposition to perceived US global dominance. Russia is feeling the longing to again be a global superpower heavyweight.

The SCO is a security bloc grouping Russia, China, and the four central Asian states of Kazakhstan, Kyrgyzstan, Tajikistan, and Uzbekistan. According to Reuters, the six members of the SCO, (Shanghai Cooperation Organization) are all against the US in a missile defense buildup in Europe. Not surprisingly, these four states are all ex-Soviet central Asian states, and continue to align themselves with Russia despite their independent status.

Russia wants to become a military superpower again and, under the guidance of the antichrist, it will have its chance to "eat its fill of flesh".

The Beast was unable to come to power until all of its body parts are present and intact. This is the underlying reason why the political alignments across the globe such as Russia and Syria have become cohesive. The Beast mainly dominates the Middle East; therefore the 'body' of the Beast is a leopard, the Muslim Middle Eastern Community. It is the reason why all of Europe has joined into a single 'bloc', and the Middle East has freed itself from all the shackles of the outside world; the entire body, from head to toe must come together before the Beast can rule. This was impossible, prior to 1933, as all of the heads had not come into being before the rise of the Nazi machine. The Beast, since the dawn of the Arab uprisings, has finally assimilated its body, and it is the last Beast to come to power before the return of Christ. We are closer to the end than any generation before us, with more knowledge at our disposal of biblical prophecy than any prior age in Christianity.

"Even so, when you see all these things, you know that it is near, right at the door." (Matthew 24:33)

The Eighth King

In the latter part of their reign,

when rebels have become completely wicked,

a stern-faced king, a master of intrigue, will arise.

-Daniel 8:23

Chapter 5

Part I

Roots of the Eighth King

*'It is not surprising that Hitler went to such lengths to hide his
past. 'The man who dreamt of a new master race was himself
descended from a family of peasants."– Ralf Jan, German author
and researcher of Adolf Hitler's ancestry*

It has been amusing to read others (sometimes
ludicrous) ideas as to the identity of the antichrist
throughout the years. He has been labeled as
personages such as US presidents past and present,
the pope (the most popular guess), and foreign heads
of state to name a few. Another wild guess is that the
antichrist will be a woman, which is an unscriptural
viewpoint; as is the pope, for the pope and any
affiliates of the Roman Catholic Church is defined in
scriptures as the "Harlot", which *is* a woman. The
antichrist will most definitely be male, and is not only
referred to as "he" but also as a "king", which is
masculine, as opposed to "Queen", which would be
feminine. My hope is that this chapter will help to
dispel the outrageous notions of this coming future
embodiment of evil; as the true church is called to be
"watchmen", meaning we should know who or what to
watch for, instead of speculation centered around pop

culture figures, as the antichrist will be mostly unknown until he is "revealed". Christians, usually with good intentions, have done harm to the gospel by making wild guesses and date setting, and has led to real prophecy being ridiculed by secular society. It is the equivalent of the little boy who cried "wolf" so many times, that when the wolf finally appeared no one believed him. The story of the antichrist is more than a Hollywood production or pure sensationalism, he will be a real man who will come to power, and the horrors that follow will be like nothing the world could have ever imagined.

We have previously examined the empires of the past, including the Greek Empire under Alexander the Great. To recapitulate, his kingdom was divided into four parts and given to his four Generals as Alexander died without an heir. Those four dynasties were the Seleucids in the Middle East, the Ptolemy in Egypt, the Lysimachus in Thrace, and the Cassander in Macedonia (Greece).

Daniel, while still in Babylon, has visions concerning these empires as was briefly discussed in another chapter. In the vision, Daniel saw himself in the citadel of Susa in the province of Elam beside the Ulai Canal, which is in present day Iran.

I looked up and there before me was a ram with two horns, standing beside the canal, and the horns were long. One of the horns was longer than the other but grew up toward the west and the north and the south. No animal could stand against him, and none could rescue from his power. He did as he pleased and became great. (Daniel 8:3-4)

The ram represented the ancient Mede/Persian Empire, the horn that grew up longer represented the Persians and the shorter horn represented the Medes.

As I was thinking about this, suddenly a goat with a prominent horn between his eyes came from the west, crossing the whole earth without touching the ground. He came toward the two-horned ram I had seen standing beside the canal and charged at him in great rage. I saw him attack the ram furiously, striking the ram and shattering his two horns. The ram was powerless to stand against him; the goat knocked him to the ground and trampled on him, and none could rescue the ram from his power. (Daniel 8:5-7)

The shaggy goat represented the kingdom of Greece, and the prominent horn was the first king, Alexander the Great. This was confirmed by an angel who gave Daniel an interpretation of his vision in Daniel 8:20-21.

The goat became very great, but at the height of his power his large horn was broken off, and in its place four prominent horns grew up toward the four winds of heaven. Out of one of them came another horn, which started small, but grew in power to the south, and to the east and toward the Beautiful Land. It grew until it reached the host of the heavens and it threw some of the starry host down to the earth and trampled on them. It set itself up to be as great as the Prince of the host; it took away the daily sacrifice from him and the place of his sanctuary was brought low. (Daniel 8:8-11)

These verses take the reader from the time of Alexander the Great, into the times of his four ruling Generals that held their kingdoms until they were conquered by the Roman Empire, and then further into a time of the future when another ruler emerges from those ancient kingdoms. Comparing the verse above to Daniel 7:8 which states, *"While I was thinking about the horns, there before me was another horn, a little one, which came up among them and three of the first horns were uprooted before it."*; the two "small horns" are one and the same. The difference between the two verses is the little horn of Daniel 7:8, is seen after the compilation of the last four empires as it should be; whereas, in Daniel 8:9 the small horn is shown emerging from its original origins, which is the Greco Empire of Alexander's four Generals. The four original horns were the four dynasties that emerged from ancient Greece, including the Seleucid Dynasty. At this point, this chapter parts company with many contemporary biblical scholars. One of the four horns of the shaggy goat *was* the Seleucid Empire, which included the Seleucid ruler, Antiochus Epiphanes. Many biblical scholars feel that the small horn that emerged from these four horns was Antiochus Epiphanes. There are two biblical verses that prove this is not the case; the first was already mentioned, that he is included in the four original horns; the second is the following verses:

In the latter part of their reign, when rebels have become completely wicked, a stern-faced king, a master of intrigue, will arise. He will become very strong, but not by his own power. He will cause astounding devastation and will succeed in whatever he does. He will destroy the mighty men and the holy people. He will cause deceit to prosper, and he will consider himself superior. When they feel secure, he will destroy many and take his stand against the Prince of princes. Yet he will be destroyed, but not by human power. (Daniel 8:23-25)

Antiochus Epiphanes was in power over Judea as part of the Seleucid Dynasty in 167 BC; he would not have been physically able to take his stand against the "Prince of Princes", as Jesus had not yet been born. Antiochus died in 164 BC and had been decomposing for more than a century at the birth of Christ. The verses from Chapter 8:23-25 were a description by the angel of a future "stern faced king" that arises from one of the four horns, and describes the time as:

"What will happen later, in the time of wrath, because the vision concerns the appointed time of the end." (Daniel 8:19)

Antiochus Epiphanes (Greek Translation=God Manifest) was a monster in his own right; he caused many problems for Judea in regards to their worship, and he took away the daily sacrifice from them, he also sacrificed a pig on the altar in the Jewish temple. When the Jews mistakenly thought Antiochus had been killed during his campaign in Egypt, they formed a revolt and ousted the high priest, Menelaus that had been installed by Antiochus in Jerusalem. Upon hearing of the revolt, Antiochus, in a fit of rage, stormed back to Jerusalem and a massacre ensued leaving 80,000 Jews dead. However, history reveals him as rather bumbling. He was unknowingly referred to by associates as Antiochus "Epimanes" a wordplay on Epiphanes, which means "mad" as he would visit locales and engage commoners in conversation, and often frequented public bath houses, which was behavior unbefitting a king; furthermore, he tried to conquer Egypt, and the Romans turned him around after humiliating him by drawing the famous line in the sand, which is where that phrase comes from. While he was dealing with the problems in Judea, King Mithradates I of Parthia took advantage of this and captured the city of Herat in 167 BC, which cut off a direct trade route to India. Antiochus left a commander in charge to handle the Jewish problem and departed Judea to deal with the new threat himself. While he was away on this campaign, the Jews resumed the Maccabean Revolt, which they ultimately won as Antiochus died before a final return to Judea to quell the revolt. He could not exactly claim that *"he prospered in everything he did"* nor can he claim that he *"reached the host of heavens and threw some of the starry host down to earth"*. The following verses give further insight into how powerful the stern faced king, "the little horn" will "prosper in everything it does", as opposed to Antiochus whom failed at conquering Egypt and was humiliated by the Romans:

Because of rebellion, the host of the saints, and the daily sacrifice were given over to it. It prospered in everything it did, and truth was thrown to the ground. (Daniel 8:12)

The 'little horn' is the first mention of the future "man of lawlessness" in the book of Daniel; it is with that point in mind that any further reference to the "stern faced king" should be based upon the fact that he has been identified as a future ruler, and not an historical one. The circumstances surrounding "the little horn" parallel enough with the actions of Antiochus Epiphanes to give the bible reader pause, as the *stern faced king* mimics the abusive conduct of the long dead ruler in a future time.

Compare the following verses, and we will find the identity of the stern faced king:

Then another sign appeared in heaven: an enormous red dragon with seven heads and ten horns and seven crowns on his heads. His tail swept a third of the stars out of the sky and flung them to the earth. (Revelation 12:3-4)

137

It grew until it reached the host of the heavens and <u>it threw some</u>
<u>of the starry host down to the earth and trampled on them.</u> It set
itself up to be as great as the Prince of the host; it took away the
daily sacrifice from him and the place of his sanctuary was
brought low. (Daniel 8:10)

The identity of the eighth king is a head on the
enormous red dragon, the seven-headed monster,
none other than Satan during his final reign on earth.
Satan gives the eighth king his power, and the eighth
king is one of the previous seven heads; therefore, they
are one and the same. Consider the conversation that
Satan had with Jesus during his trial of temptation:

Again the devil took him to a very high mountain and showed him
all the kingdoms of the world and their splendor. "All of this I will
give you", he said "if you will bow down and worship me."
(Matthew 4:8-9)

The kingdoms of the world belong to Satan at the
present time, and they did so in the time of Jesus as
well. They will continue to belong to Satan until Christ
returns to earth and sets up his kingdom during his
millennial reign. The antichrist is merely a puppet of
Satan in his final effort to defeat God.

From ancient origins to modern DNA; in determining
the origins of the future antichrist that will be of either
Mediterranean or Middle Eastern descent, a recent
article has exposed new information on the deceased
leader of the Nazi regime. The article is from an Israeli
digital newspaper, *Haaretz,* released on April 4, 2013,
that states:

Adolf Hitler may have owed more to the 'subhuman' races he tried to exterminate than to his 'Aryan' compatriots, according to new finding published in Belgium this week. In research for the Flemish-language magazine Knack, journalist Jean-Paul Mulders traced Hitler's living relatives in the Fuhrer's native Austria, as well as the United States. "The results of this study are surprising," said Ronny Decorte, a geneticist interviewed by Knack. "Hitler would not have been happy." Geneticists identify groups of chromosomes called haplogroups, 'genetic fingerprints' that define populations. According to Mulders, Hitler's dominant haplogroup, E1b1b, is relatively rare in Western Europe - but strongest in some 25 percent of Greeks and Sicilians, who apparently acquired the genes from Africa: Between 50 percent and 80 percent of North Africans share Hitler's dominant group, which is especially prevalent among in the Berber tribes of Morocco, Algeria and Tunisia, and Somalis. More surprising still, perhaps, is that Hitler's second most dominant haplogroup is the most common in Ashkenazi Jews.

This news should not be surprising considering that, though Austrian born, Hitler appeared of Mediterranean or Middle Eastern descent, and his origins would need to be of those ethnic groups, as the origins of the antichrist must derive from one of the four horns of the shaggy goat. The only plausible horn would have been the Seleucid dynasty, comprised of Greek rulers and citizens who intermarried with the native Arabic peoples of the region. The Africans that share these genes are not black, but of light-skinned Arabic origins. Confirmation of Hitler's DNA is important, as he is the number one contestant for the position of the eighth king, and he must meet all the criteria markers.

Part II
The Throne of the Antichrist

One must understand the origins of the antichrist in order to identify where he will come from. Now that we have established that he is the "little horn" that will come from the roots of the ancient Grecian Empire, we must identify which of the four dynasties he will come from.

The people of the ruler who will come will destroy the city and the sanctuary. The end will come like a flood: War will continue until the end, and desolations have been decreed. He will confirm a covenant with many for one seven. In the middle of the seven he will put an end to sacrifice and offering. And on a wing of the temple he will set up an abomination that causes desolation, until the end that is decreed is poured out on him. (Daniel 9:26-27)

These verses are mostly uncontested by all bible expositors in that this is in reference to a future ruler. The key statement in his identity is "people of the ruler who will come". We know that the city of Jerusalem and the temple were destroyed by the Roman army, Titus destroyed the temple in 70 AD and the Emperor Hadrian destroyed the city in 135 AD. However, the people who actually did the destroying were people incorporated into the Roman Legions through the nations they conquered; in other words, they weren't Roman, only a part of the Roman Empire. History

141

reveals the answer as the Romans kept very detailed records of their Legions. The answer lies in which Legions attacked Jerusalem:

Macedonia V – Garrisoned in Macedonia (Greece)

Fulminata XII – in Melitene (Turkey) Cappadocia

Apollinaris XV – in Satal (Saddagh, Turkey) but garrisoned in Syria

Fetensis X –in Jerusalem, but previously garrisoned in Syria

With the exception of Greece, the rest of the Legions were from the Middle East, namely Syria and Turkey. Both of those regions were under the Seleucid Dynasty. His origins (or place of birth) will be either Greece itself, or Middle Eastern in Syria or Turkey. The seat or power base of the Seleucid Dynasty was in Syria; however, the actual ancient rulers were born in Greece.

The most revealing scriptures that give insight as to where the antichrist's seat of power will be can be found in Revelation; Jesus' message to one of the seven churches in Revelation in the city of Pergamum:

I know where you live-where Satan has his throne. (Revelation 2:13)

Combined with the scripture:

The dragon gave the beast his power and his throne and great authority. (Revelation 13:2)

The church of Pergamum was located in what is now modern Turkey, close to the coast of the Aegean Sea. Pergamum means "Fortress"; one attribute of the antichrist is that *"He will honor a god of fortresses"* Daniel 11:38. Istanbul in Turkey was the capital of the last dynasty of the Caliphates, the Ottoman Empire. The words of Jesus tell us that the throne of Satan on the physical planet earth is in Pergamum, or Turkey and he hands it over to the antichrist during the last seven years of the tribulation. The antichrist is in control of the "revived Roman Empire", however, half of that empire is in the Middle East, or east of Rome as was discussed in the chapter *Leviathan*; his seat of power will be where he comes to power at, which will be in the regions of Turkey and Syria, and both were assimilated as part of the 'Assyrian Empire' in the ancient world long before the Seleucid Dynasty came into being. This Middle Eastern location is not new information, some of the earliest Christian scholars came to the same conclusions while deciphering the scriptures in reference to the location of the future antichrist; but throughout the ages their historical references have been all but lost to modern scholars.

It is interesting to note that the distinguished premillennialist, Theodore Zahn, states (c. 1900) that the final evil ruler in Revelation (much of which is based on Daniel) is "without question" derived from "the Greco-Macedonian [kingdom] and its typical pre-Christian antichrist, Antiochus Epiphanes" (Introduction to the New Testament, Vol. III, p. 441). In Daniel 11 and 12 it seems clear that Antiochus is a "type" of the yet future tyrant. Antiochus was a Syrian king. A Latin church father, Lactantius (c. 250-330 AD), clearly expected the Beast [antichrist] to arise in Syria: "Another king shall arise out of Syria, born from an evil spirit,...and he will constitute and call himself God, and will order himself to be worshipped as the Son of God, and power will be given him to do signs and wonders. Then he will attempt to destroy the temple of God and persecute the righteous people; and there will be distress and tribulation such as there never has been since the beginning of the world" (Divine Institutes, Book 7, ch. 17). In ch. 16 Lactantius speaks of the tyrant arising "from the extreme boundaries of the northern region." Another ante-Nicene father, Victorinus (c. 280 AD) refers Micah 5:5 to the antichrist: "There shall be peace for our land...and they shall encircle Assur [Assyria], that is antichrist, in the trench of Nimrod" (Commentary on the Apocalypse, 7th chapter). Assyria is the approximate equivalent of modern Iraq. Victorinus also speaks of Babylon as the Roman state

- Anthony Buzzard, Focus on the Kingdom

The term "fortress" has been erroneously misinterpreted as referring to a military compound or a siege of war, however, it is indicated specifically in Daniel 11:31 that it refers to first the Jewish temple, and second, in Daniel 11:39 a vague reference to the "mightiest fortresses" which implicates other religions, such as the Vatican. The usage of the word "fortress" in scriptures has a deeper significance as well, the events of war portrayed in Daniel and Revelation are related to *Holy* or *Religious* wars, as the term fortress is used when describing the attack from the man of lawlessness. We know that he attacks and destroys the Vatican; he also desecrates the Jewish temple at the midpoint of the tribulation, so the implications of him plotting to attack other fortresses are probably due to a religious affiliation. There are scriptures that confirm why he feels it necessary to attack other religious institutions; he exalts himself as God, and anyone not adhering to him being worshiped is annihilated, thus we find the reason for the beheaded saints; "*He will show no regard for the gods of his fathers or for the one desired by women, nor will he regard any god, but will exalt himself above them all."* The countries and religions therein that do not worship him as God will be destroyed or will go to war against him, including the countries of the Far East and perhaps others not mentioned in scripture such as India; we find verses in Revelation that correlate to this explanation;

He ordered them to set up an image in honor of the beast who was wounded by the sword and yet lived. He was given power to give breath to the image of the first beast, so that it could speak and cause all who refused to worship the image to be killed. (Revelation 13:14-15)

He also forced everyone, small and great, rich and poor, free and slave, to receive a mark on his right hand or on his forehead, so that no one could buy or sell unless he had the mark, which is the name of the beast or the number of his name. (Revelation 13:16-17)

It said to the sixth angel who had the trumpet, 'Release the four angels who are bound at the great river Euphrates'. And the four angels who had been kept ready for this very hour and day and month and year were released to kill a third of mankind. The number of the mounted troops was two hundred million. I heard their number. (Revelation 9:14)

The sixth angel poured out his bowl on the great river Euphrates, and its water was dried up to prepare the way for the kings from the East. (Revelation 16:12.)

Those verses are depicting the 'Battle of Armageddon', in which many countries come against the antichrist when he is based in Israel. They converge on the plain of Megiddo in northern Israel including the Kings of the East meaning Asian in origin, China, Japan, North and South Korea, Vietnam, etc. The Far East has mostly been separated from the rest of the world throughout antiquity to present day. They have their own customs, and though they have profited from trade with other nations, they do not usually get involved in major world affairs with the exception of World War II, that being Japan only. Through the lens of the preceding verses we see the Asian continent cut off from trade unless they worship the beast; followed by the whole of Asia coming together en masse against the new world leader. Religion has caused more wars than politics throughout history, and this case will be no different, except in scope and magnitude of the battle that ensues. The Asian army will kill one third of mankind during this battle with 200 million in their fighting ranks. Israel is a small country, and the plain of Megiddo is even smaller, yet 200 million troops from Asia will be there, not including the armies of the antichrist, mainly Arabic, and many other troops from other countries. They will literally be shoulder to shoulder like sardines in a can, this is the reason why the blood from the dead soldiers will be as high as a horses' bridle (about 4 feet high) and flowed to a distance of about 180 miles; *"They were trampled in winepress outside the city, and blood flowed out of the press, rising as high as the horses' bridles for a distance of 1,600 stadia (about 300 kilometers)"* (Revelation 14:20)

In Daniel 11:39 it states, *"He will attack the mightiest fortresses with the help of a foreign god and will greatly honor those who acknowledge him."* The use of the phrase "foreign god" leaves the reader questioning, foreign to whom? What perspective is it being labeled "foreign", from an Angelic, Arabic, European or Judaic (such as Daniel) perspective? Or from a human perspective, and the foreign god is of a demonic nature? We have confirmed that his main followers are Arabic, those who adhere to Islam, while he possibly being Middle Eastern by birth origin could not call 'Allah' foreign, yet he seems to try and obliterate all other religions including Christianity. The verse implies he receives help from a foreign god, possibly meaning the god of the people used in combat to attack other fortresses, however the verse is very vague in nature and only the actual events will confirm what the true meaning is. When the church witnesses these events, hopefully, many of the saints will recognize the time they are living in, and instruct others as to who will be sitting on the Middle Eastern throne as he is revealed to the church.

Part III
Revealing the Man of Lawlessness

Don't let anyone deceive you in any way, for that day will not come, until the falling away (apostasy) occurs and the man of lawlessness is revealed, the man doomed to destruction. (2 Thessalonians 2:3)

In the early church, a rumor had started that the Christians Paul preached to, had missed the Lord's coming. Paul, not wanting them to be alarmed, gave the Church of Thessalonica certain guidelines to be aware of for the time of the end. Those guidelines across the span of 2,000 years seem to have been misplaced by many Christians, theologians, and pastors. It is the subject of the "rapture", and in today's evangelical circles; unfortunately, it is a volatile subject of much debate and contention. The biblical viewpoint for the "catching up" of the saints does not support a pre-apocalyptic or pre-tribulation view; that is a fact and is supported by scriptures. One of the main scriptures that Pre-Tribulation rapture theorists use is found in Thessalonians when speaking of the antichrist to come:

Don't you remember that when I was with you, I used to tell you these things? And now you know what is holding him back, so that he may be revealed at the proper time. For the secret power of lawlessness is already at work; but the one who now holds it back will continue to do so till he is taken out of the way. And then the

148

lawless one will be revealed, whom the Lord Jesus will overthrow with the breath of his mouth and destroy by the splendor of his coming. (2 Thessalonians 2:5-8)

Their argument is the church and/or Holy Spirit is holding him back, therefore the church must be raptured before he can be revealed. Yet, in the same chapter in verse 2:3, Paul states that *"our being gathered to him cannot occur until the apostasy occurs and the man of lawlessness if revealed"*. The church cannot be removed and still be here for the man of lawlessness to be revealed. One statement cancels out the other. The entire Pre-tribulation rapture theory is unscriptural, and creates confusion for the church; this book does not debate "the pre-trib rapture theory", as it would be a discredit to the very words of Jesus, however, the facts of the events preceding the actual rapture of the church are stated. The "pre-trib" believers are waiting to be "raptured" instead of watching and being prepared. In a biology class, it was taught that a person can place a live frog in a pot of water on the stove and slowly heat it up and the frog will never try to jump out, even to the point of being boiled to death. That will be the "pre-trib rapture group" of the church during the tribulation, they won't believe we are at the time of the end because they "absolutely know" we will be raptured away first. They will ignore the signing of the 'Peace Treaty' between the man of lawlessness and Israel, and discard it as just another happening in the Middle East. Jesus expressed that we are to be prepared and watching for his return, stating that he would return as a thief in the night. The scriptures also state that a great apostasy would occur before his return, and in fact described what the apostasy would look like. The apostasy occurs immediately before the Antichrist is 'revealed', and the apostasy described by Jesus in

Revelation 3:15-17 is to the "Laodicean" church. *"I know your deeds, that you are neither cold nor hot. I wish you were either one or the other! So because you are lukewarm-neither hot nor cold-I am about to spit you out of my mouth. You say 'I am rich; I have acquired wealth and do not need a thing.' But you do not realize that you are wretched, pitiful, poor, blind and naked."* It appears that another gospel is being preached before the immediate unveiling of the Man of Sin; this gospel is not about salvation, but about wealth, or to use another word, "prosperity". Those accusations are made by Jesus himself, our Lord. The gospel of prosperity states "What will God do for you if you do (or give) to God". The minority of pastors that preach against this doctrine are unfairly accused of envy and jealousy because the mega churches are doing so well. The argument lacks logic, as a pastor that was indeed only envious need only to begin preaching prosperity and his church would split their seems. Preaching to congregations regarding God's favor for his people is not wrong, however when it is the only doctrine available, one needs to question the motive. The truly regrettable part is that a majority of the pastors that have grown these huge ministries began humbly and with great zeal for the message, and somehow lost their way, and quite possibly their crown. When some of these pastors are interviewed by secular journalists, they are often asked questions that in their answer reveal that they hold not to the original biblical doctrine. Questions such as "Is Jesus the only path to heaven?", and "Are homosexuals going to hell?" In today's society, being politically correct means a much larger bankroll to a mega church. Some pastors that were interviewed have failed the test of these two basic questions that require a righteous answer in a morally bankrupt society. If a pastor or Christian does not call "sin" a "sin" what makes the church different than the secular world? They gave the cowardly answer of "I'm

150

not here to judge"; and they most likely will not in the kingdom of God either. They were basically asked a question of what they believe, they were not being asked to stone an adulterer. And yes, Jesus is the only path to heaven (John 14:6); and yes, homosexuality is a sin and they will spend eternity in hell if they do not repent of their fleshly lust (Genesis 19:1-29, Leviticus 20:13, Romans 1:26-28, 1 Corinthians 6:9-10). It would not be love to spare a person's carnal feelings and have them spend eternity separated from God when it could have been prevented with the truth. It is this 'politically correct' scratch an itching ear style of worship that is prevalent and which will lead up to the Antichrist being revealed. This information was revealed to us through the message to the Laodicean Church in Asia Minor in which Jesus described the apostasy; it is not an apostasy of believers leaving the church and converting to atheism, it is the 'wealth' of the church and the reason the congregation is there. This exhibits an apathy for the true word of God and the message of the gospel; Jesus states *"At that time many will turn away from the faith and will betray and hate each other"* (Matthew 24:10). When a person comes into church and is taught health, wealth and prosperity only and then is faced with a decision of choosing Jesus and being put to death or denying him and living, he will feel as though the church was a 'scam' because he was never taught anything beyond what God would do for him. The mission of a pastor is to win souls with the whole truth of the bible; however, the mega churches are more concerned with winning congregation numbers. Jesus states "I know your deeds", meaning 'works'; this implies that they have many works and ministries through these churches, but Jesus is implying that they are neither hot or cold, in other words, works of apathy.

In Jesus' tribulation discourse in Mathew 24:4-31; he gives an explanation of the signs that will occur before his coming, and he is explicit. He begins with the statement *"Watch out that no one deceives you"*...some believers are being deceived by a pre-tribulation rapture theory. He states that there will be wars, rumors of wars, famines and earthquakes, which is all the beginning of birth pains. He goes on to describe how some believers will be persecuted and martyred, and the church shall see the *abomination of desolation* standing in the holy place, he then ends his discourse with the following verse:

Immediately following the distress of those days, "the sun will be darkened, and the moon will not give its light; the stars will fall from the sky, and the heavenly bodies will be shaken." At that time the sign of the Son of Man will appear in the sky, and all the nations of the earth will mourn. They will see the Son of Man coming on the clouds of the sky, with power and great glory. And he will send his angels with a loud trumpet call, and they will gather his elect from the four winds, from one end of the heavens to the other (Matthew 24:29-31)

And if the words of Jesus are not enough to convince the most avid pre-tribbers, compare the trumpet call scriptures:

We who are still alive, who are left to the coming of the Lord, will certainly not precede those who have fallen asleep. For the Lord himself will come down from heaven, with a loud command, with voice of the archangel and with the trumpet call of God, and the dead in Christ will rise first. After that, we who are still alive and are left will be caught up together with them in the clouds to meet the Lord in the air. (1 Thessalonians 4:15-17)

Listen, I tell you a mystery; we will not all sleep. But we will all be changed in a flash, in the twinkling of an eye, <u>at the last trumpet</u>. (Corinthians 15:52)

Which trumpet is the last trumpet? Revelation tells us there are a total of seven trumpets:

<u>The seventh angel sounded his trumpet</u>, and there were loud voices in heaven, which said "the kingdom of the world has become the kingdom of our Lord and of his Christ and he will reign forever and ever" (Revelation 11:15)

It is important to understand that the Christians who are alive at the time of the end will see and experience the real "apocalypse", and should be able to recognize the man of lawlessness. It is also important to understand how the bible views prophecy and prophetic events.

Tongues, then, are a sign, not for believers but for unbelievers; prophecy, however, is for believers, not for unbelievers. (1 Corinthians 14:22)

My belief is that the entire book of the bible, from table of contents to maps, is the truthful living word of God. I also believe that God is powerful enough to insure that his word has been preserved in exactness of how it was originally written, and that the words of Jesus in scripture are the most important words in the entire bible. If someone has interpreted scriptures such that the interpretation does not agree with scriptures, and especially in regards to the words of Jesus, then the interpretation is incorrect, not the word of God as it is the standard of measure for absolute truth. Understanding that the rapture is presented in a way scripturally that occurs at the end of the tribulation is not a "view", but a correct interpretation of scriptures by the very words of Jesus; furthermore, it is relevant in discerning the coming events of the "man of sin." Jesus made a remark during his tribulation discourse that included a passage from Daniel:

So when you see standing in the holy place, the "abomination that causes desolation", spoken of through the prophet Daniel-let the reader understand- then let those who are in Judea flee to the mountains. (Matthew 24:15)

This is a major point of reference in determining certain characters in a specific timeframe outlined in Daniel 11:21-35; one verse in particular is Daniel 11:31, *"His armed forces will rise up to desecrate the temple fortress and will abolish the daily sacrifice. Then they will set up the abomination that causes desolation."* The phrase *"abomination of desolation and daily sacrifice being taken away"* is referred to a total of four times in Daniel, in verses 8:11-13, 9:27, 11:31, and 12:11. The angel Gabriel gives Daniel a final synopsis in verse 12:11 that summarizes the other three times the phrase is mentioned. The fact that the phrase is again mentioned by Jesus gives the reader an understanding that it is a future event from the time of Jesus's ministry. The Romans never took away the daily sacrifice from the Jewish people, and the temple being destroyed in 70 AD has prevented this event from occurring during the last 2,000 years.

The angel Gabriel sought Daniel out for a final conversation in which he explains the timeline of his people from the Persian Kings to the time of the end. In Daniel 11:2-20 he describes what we now know historically to be from the times of the Persian kings to Alexander's conquest, and then forward into the Seleucid Empire. From verse 11:21 forward is where the debate begins of "who" the king of the north is, and whether it is referring to an historical king or a future ruler. Bible expositors have done some peculiar things to the verses that begin in Daniel 11:21-12:3. The most frequent interpretation by many bible annotators beginning in verse 21, is concurring that this verse pertains to Antiochus Epiphanes, however, Antiochus did not fulfill most of the prophecies in these scriptures, unless one adlibs into history what the prophetic account entails. The only verse that would actually connect Antiochus to any of these verses is 11:31, in which this evil ruler desecrates the temple fortress, and sets up the *"abomination that causes desolation";* however, we have already surmised that this is a future event as described by Jesus himself. Another bizarre conception some biblical explicators have presented when reading the narrative straight through is to use verse 11:36 as an introduction to a third party or a "new king"; whereas the preceding verses only contain two kings, being the king of the north and the king of the south. It is clear that verse 12:11 in which the angel Gabriel states, *"From the time that the daily sacrifice is abolished and the abomination that causes desolation is set up, there will be 1,290 days"* that he is referencing the entire narrative starting from verse 11:21 through 11:45, and that it is referring to the same person, as the king of the north. The day for a year substitution cannot be used in this particular context as some historical exegetes have done, such as Isaac Newton, as the timeframe does not match any historically significant event that occurred in 1290 or 1335 years from the time spoken of from 167 BC to around 1035 AD; the Jews had been dispersed from Israel and the church had not yet encountered the tyranny from the Roman Catholic Church. The following excerpt lends an understanding to philology, which is the study of language in written historical sources such as the bible.

A distinguished professor of the Old Testament wisely said of Daniel 11:

It is contrary to all sound principles of exegesis to suppose that, in a continuous description, with no indication whatever of a change of subject, part should refer to one person and part to another, and "the king" (Dan. 11:36) should be a different king from the one whose doings are described in verses 21-35 (S.R. Driver, Commentary on Daniel, Cambridge Bible for Schools and Colleges, p. 193).

Henry Cowles, D.D., who taught the book of Daniel for 25 years to young men preparing for ministry, expressed his conviction that Daniel 11:21-45 describes the career of a single King of the North: "The bonds of philological connection are of the strongest kind. It would seem to be simply impossible for one accustomed to study, observe and obey the laws of philology, and to interpret language in view of what is, to have even the least doubt on this point" (Daniel, with Notes Critical, Explanatory and Practical, p. 448).

The professor's remarks are a pointed and much needed corrective to much exposition of Daniel 11 and remind us that we are first and foremost bound by the normal rules of language when we read the Bible. We are also bound, if we claim to be Christians, to accept the interpretation which Jesus puts on a given passage. Fortunately his express reference (Matt. 24:15) to the Abomination of Desolation found in Daniel 11:31, 12:11 (as well as 9:27) removes all doubt as to how Daniel's words are to be applied. Certainly they cannot refer to Antiochus Epiphanes (except, perhaps, as a type) when Jesus refers them to the future!

Space does not permit a demonstration of the various other attempts which have been made to insert a third power into the narrative of Daniel 11:21-45. A straightforward reading of the passage leads us to believe that the future will reveal an end-time struggle between the tyrannical King of the North (i.e., from Syria or Iraq, the northern division

of the ancient Kingdom of Greece, see Dan. 11:4-6) and the King of the
South (presumably Egypt). Inserting into the narrative powers from
other geographical regions breaks the thread of the story which formed
Daniel's crowning vision. Surely this ultimate revelation given to Daniel
and the church, as recipients of Holy Scripture, must inspire us to
vigorous evangelism before the dark days of the final enemy of God
arrive.

-Focus on the Kingdom

One of the main reasons that many exponentials support the inconclusive supposition that verse 11:36 skips forward in history to bypass the church age is that it supports a "pretribulationist" view, including a "secret" pre-tribulation rapture of the church. If the abomination of desolation in verse 11:31 is placed in antiquity, then there is no chance that the church could be included in verses 11:32-35. However, scripturally we know the *"dead in Christ rise first"* 1 Thessalonians 4:16; therefore the rapture cannot take place until after *"those who sleep in the dust awake"*. The entire passage of Daniel 11:21-12:3 should be read as a continual passage, as it was meant to be read, and either placed wholly in antiquity or in a future time. Again, the problem of placing it wholly in antiquity is the verses from 11:36 onward have yet to be fulfilled by any ruler, past or present. Therefore, the entire passage should be viewed as a future prophecy. The mainstream media of biblical exegesis in modern prophecy support the pre-tribulation rapture theory as it has become the most popular notion for today's churches. The "Left Behind" series has even secular audiences waiting for the next book in the series to be released. Believing in either view of the rapture is not relevant to salvation, and the sensationalism that comes from the media for those sources are advantageous in sharing the gospel with the secular world; however, as a serious student of biblical prophecy, one cannot entertain notions based on popularity which are unsupported by scriptures.

Where is Antiochus?

In the passages of Daniel 11 we find a small unobserved verse, "*His sons will prepare for war and assemble a great army which will sweep on like an irresistible flood and carry the battle as far as his fortress.*" (Daniel 11:10) The "sons" this verse refers to is the sons of King Antiochus III, and the entire passage from this point forward to verse 11:20 deals with the war between Egypt and the Seleucid kingdom that belonged to King Antiochus III followed by Seleucus Philopator IV and Antiochus Epiphanes, the title "king of the north" becomes interchangeable between King Antiochus III, Seleucus Philopator IV which begins in 11:15, and Antiochus Epiphanes IV; as they are all his "sons" and were acting as kings. In verse 11:18, we find Antiochus Epiphanes in Alexandria and he had already sent a fleet to capture Cyprus; "*Then he will turn his attention to the coastlands and will take many of them, but a commander will put an end to his insolence and will turn his insolence back upon him.*" (Daniel 11:18) The commander that puts an end to his insolence is Gaius Popillus, a Roman general sent by Rome to give Antiochus an ultimatum. He told Antiochus to evacuate Egypt; Antiochus, trying to buy time, said he needed to speak with his council first. Upon hearing this impudent response, the Romans drew a line in the sand around Antiochus stating that he needed to give his answer before stepping out of the circle or consider himself at war with Rome. Thoroughly insulted by the Romans, he evacuated Egypt, and slunk back towards his fortresses with his tail between his legs. The humiliation depicted by that specific verse is where the famous saying "draw a line in the sand" comes from. Antiochus was the only Seleucid king to receive such an insult, and the saying is still used today as a form of referring to an ultimatum. Upon his death, a tax collector was sent out, as his kingdom was left to his infant son under guardianship, however, Rome was in power and defeated the Seleucid kingdom before his son was old enough to act as king. Those historical facts match the passage from 11:10 through 11:20; thereby leaving 11:21 open to a future ruler that succeeds the throne of the ancient Seleucid kingdom. It also corresponds to the words of Jesus in Matthew 24:15 in which he points to a future time in which the abomination of desolation is carried out, causing the people in Israel to flee to the mountains. Another point of reference in which bible expositors, when studying these verses prior to the year 1945, would only have had an historical perspective in that it was fulfilled in antiquity, as the Jewish nation had ceased to exist in Israel. Time is the key that has unlocked Daniel without having to guess at an outcome, as we now know that Israel has become a nation again, and thereby can flee to the mountains when the abomination becomes a reality.

Part IV
The Son of Perdition

Perdition: A state of eternal punishment and damnation into which a sinful and unpenitent person passes after death, a state of final spiritual ruin; loss of the soul; damnation, the future state of the wicked.

The antichrist is called "The Son of Perdition" (2 Thessalonians 2:3). The Holy Scriptures oppose what transpires after death in the natural world by the resurrection of the dead. Perdition, by definition, is a state of the human soul *after death*, yet the antichrist is called the son of perdition. The very definition tells us that this man is indeed brought back to life from the dead. Upon entering the abyss, he entered perdition, eternally damned. He could not be called "son" unless he had passed through death into the abyss. His return from the abyss is not as a regenerated soul, but the same one only condemned to perdition. He does not appear on earth a second time as a normal person who chooses to go astray, but wicked from the moment he arrives. He feels that he should be worshiped as a deity, the only deity on the planet as a risen savior.

We know from scriptures that everyone on the planet who has ever lived here will be resurrected one day, some to everlasting righteousness and some to eternal damnation. The concept of the resurrection of the dead is prevalent throughout scriptures; it is the basis of a Christian's hope in eternal life. However, the concept of raising a dead evil dictator seems absurd. According to historical sources, Hitler's body was burned after committing suicide. The flesh of any human cannot pass into heaven or hell, therefore upon his death, his soul went into perdition. Much the same as the spirit of Elijah in John the Baptist, the spirit of the final antichrist will inhabit a different body. Paul spoke of the Man of Lawlessness being "revealed", it is this revealing of who he was that astonishes the world. He reveals himself by stating he is god while standing inside the Holy of Holies. The bible does not teach reincarnation, as John the Baptist was identified as having the spirit of Elijah, and was even called Elijah by Jesus; John himself denied that he was Elijah. Elijah never died, being caught up to heaven in a whirlwind, and Elisha wanted a double portion of his spirit. In conjecture, the situation with the antichrist is more difficult to understand, as the scriptures clearly confirm that he is a man that has returned from the dead, and as a man that has died, he is entitled to a resurrection at some point. We know that immediately following the return of Christ, the beast and the false prophet are thrown into the lake of fire; therefore, they get no resurrection later at judgment, as Christ judges them immediately. One can speculate that this one event is the antichrist's one allotted resurrection, and the false prophet had never died, therefore he is judged at the coming of Christ.

Comparison of Antiochus to the Coming Antichrist

Through this section, we will assimilate the historical facts of the controversial passage in Daniel to discover the true meaning of the scripture, and draw a conclusion for this passage that indicates the events are portrayed in a future timeframe.

Daniel 11:21-27

(11:21) He will be succeeded by a contemptible person who has not been given the honor of royalty.

Antiochus Epiphanes was a legitimate son of King Antiochus III and Queen Laodice. He was a full blooded prince from a long line of Kings in the Seleucid Dynasty. The antichrist will be an anonymous person from obscurity, thus he must be "revealed". When he is revealed, he will be instantly recognized by the entire world; *"The whole world was astonished and followed the beast."* (Revelation 13:3)

(11:21) He will invade the kingdom when its people feel secure, and he will seize it through intrigue.

Antiochus inherited the entire empire of the Seleucid Dynasty, although his methods for obtaining the throne were questionable, as he supposedly killed his infant nephew which was the next heir apparent, he was still a legitimate successor. He also had no need to invade his own kingdom; when he took control of the kingdom he had no need to use flattery, which could occur if he were being "voted" in, but as a successor to the throne, he did not need the agreement of the people to take control.

(11:22)Then an overwhelming army will be swept away before him, both it and a prince of the covenant will be destroyed.

Neither of these occurred when Antiochus came to power, neither his army, nor the Egyptian Army was "swept away", and a prince of the covenant, which would have been a Jewish leader of Israel, was not destroyed either.

(11:26) His army will be swept away, and many will fall in battle.

This verse is connected to verse 22 above; it is the same army and refers to the Egyptian army. The Egyptian army during the course of Antiochus' reign was never swept away, which means destroyed. When Antiochus invaded Egypt the first time, he won politically as his nephew was on the throne and he tried to use him to gain control of Egypt, without alarming the Romans.

(11:23) After coming to an agreement with him, he will act deceitfully, and with only a few people he will rise to power.

The verse infers to an agreement with the prince of the host in verse 22 that is swept away along with the Egyptian army. Antiochus never made an agreement with the Jewish people; they had no leverage with him, and when they rebelled, he massacred them. When combining this passage with Daniel 9:27, *"He will confirm a covenant with many for one seven. In the middle of the seven he will put an end to sacrifice and offering."* It flows amiably, as the verses in chapter 9 refer to the future ruler; and even describes the details of how he acts deceitfully, by reneging on his earlier agreement. Another point of reference is that Antiochus never had to rise to power; he inherited the entire kingdom of his father, King Antiochus III.

(11:24) When the richest provinces feel secure, he will invade them and will achieve what neither his fathers nor his forefathers did. He will distribute, plunder, loot and wealth among his followers. He will plot the overthrow of fortresses but only for a time.

He never invaded his own kingdom as he inherited it. Province, as used in this sentence, refers to a geographical location inside a country, as opposed to another country. The verse implies he invaded cities of great wealth within his own country (which would have been Syria), Antiochus was only interested in Egypt; this was also in no way implying that Judea was a province, as during the course of the passage, Judea is referred to as "the Beautiful Land", thus separating it from other any other geographical location. Antiochus has never been recorded as distributing wealth of any kind, and with history's accuracy into his character (such as calling him "mad") it certainly would have been recorded should he have had that kind of success militarily or if he had been that generous to his constituents. He also was not one overly eager to invade foreign lands, with the exception of Egypt, and seemed content to hold onto his father's kingdom. Plotting the overthrow of fortresses seems to refer to a character that is more inclined to expand their empire more so than Antiochus was.

> *Verses 25 through 31 are verses that could be construed as occurring during the course of Antiochus' reign, so we will skip forward to verse 32.*

(11:32) With flattery he will corrupt those who have violated the covenant, but the people who know their God will firmly resist him.

What covenant? The covenant is the holy covenant, it is alluded to in verse 28; however, it is referred to explicitly in chapter 9:27 as the future ruler to confirm a covenant for one "seven". The covenant of Israel was never in question when Antiochus ruled Judea; the Jews had remained in their homeland for hundreds of years since the Babylonian exile, unlike today when the entire world cries out "Land for peace!", and constantly reminds the Jews that the land they live on belongs to Arabs.

(11:33) Those who are wise will instruct many though for a time they will fall by the sword or be burned or captured or plundered.

The wise and unwise both fell to Antiochus' outburst of rage, however, we find another scripture in Revelation 13:10 that give us a future reference for this event perpetrated by the future evil king: *"If anyone is to go into captivity, into captivity he will go. If anyone is to be killed with the sword, with the sword he will be killed. This calls for patient endurance and faithfulness on the part of the saints."*
(11:34-35) When they fall, they will receive a little help, and many who are not sincere will join them. Some of the wise will stumble, so that they may be refined, purified and made spotless until the time of the end. For it will still come at the appointed time.

When the Jews revolted and Antiochus returned to Judea, 80,000 Jews were slaughtered in Jerusalem within 3 days. They received no help from anyone, and there certainly was no time for anyone to join them sincere or not. That equals to 27,000 Jews killed per day for 3 consecutive days. Even Hitler would have had a difficult time keeping up that pace. It goes on to say that some of the wise will stumble; the wise indicating the people who understand the significance of the situation according to prophecy. The Jews were completely unprepared for the massacre that followed their rebellion as Antiochus had thus far treated them mildly which led to their bravado, nor do orthodox Jews treat the book of Daniel as a prophetic book, as it is only included in the Old Testament as writings instead of prophecy, because of the reference to "the anointed one", Jesus; Daniel is not regarded as a Jewish prophet in Judaism. There will be many people, however, that will recognize and understand the time when the antichrist comes to power. The last statement is the *"wise are made spotless until the time of the end, for it will still come at the appointed time"*. It would be a colossal assumption that a Jewish person existing in the year 167 BC was being made spotless for the time of the end, which as of today has been more than 2,100 years into the future. As to the reference of the "time of the end", there is only one "end". It is not referring to the end of the Jewish time, or the end of the Gentiles, it is the time of the end portrayed in the events of the apocalyptic scenario in Revelation. Any biblical commentator who infers there is more than one "end" is overthinking the reference made by the angel. The bible was not written to be overly difficult to understand by those of faith, and if one is reading it through, it is pretty straight forward. Consider the following verse regarding "time of the end":

"And this gospel of the kingdom will be preached in the whole world as a testimony to all nations, and then the end will come." (Matthew 24:14)

Which "end" is Jesus referring to? He doesn't say because there is only one "end time"; it is referred to in several different phrases throughout the bible, *the end* (Matthew 24:13,14), *day of the lord* (2 Peter 3:10-13, Joel 2:28-32, Malachi 4:5), *day of wrath and wrath of the Lamb* (Zephaniah 1:15, Revelation 6:17), *the last days and day of judgment* (2 Timothy 3:1-5, 2 Peter 3:3-7), *great tribulation* (Matthew 24:21-22), and *latter days* (Micah 4:1-3,Isaiah 2:2)

Since we have determined that Antiochus Epiphanes is not the "king of the north" in verses 11:21-35, we shall look for other traits or characteristics of the coming son of perdition as the future 'king of the north'. The scriptures reveal many details of the "man of lawlessness" or the antichrist; some of the following characteristics are closely associated with him as confirmed in the correlating biblical verses:

I.   He is extremely and violently Anti-Christian and Anti-Catholic - He persecutes and martyrs the saints, and he associates the Roman Catholic Church with Christianity as a whole and eventually destroys the Vatican.

He opened his mouth to blaspheme God, and to slander his name and his dwelling place and those who live in heaven. He was given power to make war against the saints and to conquer them. (Revelation 13:6-7)

And I saw the souls of those who had been beheaded because of their testimony for Jesus and because of the word of God. They had not worshiped the beast or his image and had not received his mark on their foreheads or their hands. (Revelation 20:4)

*As I watched, this horn was waging war against
the saints and defeating them, until the Ancient of
days came and pronounced judgment in favor of
the saints of the Most High and time came when
they possessed the kingdom. (Daniel 7:21-22)*

*The beast and the ten horns you saw will hate
the prostitute. They will bring her to ruin and
leave her naked; they will eat her flesh and burn
her with fire. For God has put it into their hearts
to accomplish his purpose by agreeing to give the
beast their power to rule until God's words are
fulfilled. (Revelation 17:16-17)*

II.   He is Pro-Judaic in the beginning of his rule –
He comes to a peaceful agreement with the
modern nation of Israel, and possibly is involved
in the restoration of their temple as referred to
as a "fortress", as he adorns the temple with
costly gifts.

*He will confirm a covenant with many for one
"seven".* – Daniel 9:27, the covenant is with
Israel, and it could only be the covenant of
Abraham, in that the land of Judea belongs to
Israel. The other covenants; Adamic, Noahic,
Mosaic, and Davidic have no significant meaning
in the context of this verse.

*Instead of them, he will honor a god of fortresses;
a god unknown to his fathers he will honor with
precious stones and costly gifts.*
– Daniel 11:38, combined with *"His armed forces
will rise up to desecrate the temple fortress."* –
Daniel 11:31, these two verses imply that the
fortress of the temple that is desecrated is the
same fortress that is previously given costly gifts
by him. It is clear that his obsession is with

religious relics and temples and not the god served therein. He appears to possibly have the same infatuation with religious objects as Hitler did, and this could be the motive of his "pro-Judaism" in the beginning. He could believe that by obtaining religious relics, it will bring him victory in battle, thus his about-face towards Israel could be due to a less than victorious outcome of some future situation. It is my belief that the current nation of Israel, as well as the nation of Islam will believe that this evil imposter is their awaited Messiah; this concept will be discussed further in another chapter.

III.   He had a fatal (meaning death occurred) head wound, but is alive again.

When John first sees this beast rise from the sea, one of the peculiar things he notices is that one of the heads on the monster had a fatal wound which means he had been killed, yet the head had come back to life. *"One of the heads of the beast seemed to have had a fatal wound, but the fatal wound had been healed"* – Revelation 13:3. This eliminates the antichrist being fatally wounded after he comes to power, which explains why everyone who sees him is completely astonished; they are seeing a dead man that has been brought back to life. *"The whole world was astonished and followed the beast. Men worshiped the dragon because he had given great authority to the beast and asked "Who is like the beast? Who can make war against him?"* Who could possibly fight against a man who had been raised from the grave? The entire scenario is a counterfeit miracle mimicking Jesus, the risen Lord. Satan's plan from the very beginning has been to deceive mankind; he began his deception campaign in the Garden of Eden and has been trying to lure man in the opposite direction of God ever since. Satan has an old bag of tricks and he continues to use the same ones repeatedly, only disguised with a new face in a new time.

IV.   The antichrist will not be of royal birth or nobility, nor does he have a claim to any throne. He comes from an obscure background with a lineage of no importance. He is one of the previous heads of the beast; therefore history can confirm the lineage of the previous rulers of the heads, keeping in mind only one ruler can fulfill all the prophetic pronouncements.

He will be succeeded by a contemptible person who has not been given the honor of royalty. (Daniel 11:21)

V.   The known criteria that correlates the eighth king to the Nazi regime under Adolf Hitler:

1. Hitler was opposed to the Catholic Church and Christianity in general; he made many disparaging remarks about Christians and he felt that religion was for the weak.

2. He was obsessed with religious objects such as the spear of destiny, and deeply immersed in the occult.

3. The fact that he was extremely anti-Semitic, and the antichrist will be pro-Semitic is opposing, however it could work in his favor that he had a change of heart from his "death experience" by agreeing to a covenant for seven years, and

could also explain why he adorns their temple with gifts; political moves to foster trust.

4. The most important factor, he died from a fatal head wound, a gunshot wound to the head. The Nazi party essentially died with him.

5. He is the only recognizable person from all the previous rulers of past empires that would astonish the world.

6. He was born from obscurity, in a lower middle class home, his parents had to work as he did not come from a wealthy family, and his father worked in the civil service. He had no ties to royalty or nobility. British monarchs must be born into royalty to take the throne, the Vatican selects the popes into succession and had a series of popes during its imperial years, the Roman empire was led by men who were of noble birth as they used a class system, the Greeks of the four dynasties were all from a lineage of kings and Alexander's father was a king, the Mede/Persians were all kings with lineages that can be traced to ancient Mesopotamia and Babylon the same. Hitler and his Nazi regime is the only candidate that can fulfill that particular prophecy exactly.

Part V
The Beginning of the End

After coming to an agreement with him, he will act deceitfully and with only a few people he will rise to power. (Daniel 11:23)

The agreement is between the antichrist and the prince of the covenant or Jewish leader/ruler. This has yet to be fulfilled, and the verse infers that the antichrist needs this agreement to be able to rise to power.

The two kings, with their hearts bent on evil, will sit at the same table and lie to each other but to no avail, because an end will still come at the appointed time. (Daniel 11:27)

It is an odd sentence that seems to have no business in a biblical passage. The reason is, it was not fulfilled in antiquity, but is to come. Today a table is not just for dining, it is used for heads of state to sit and discuss their politics as can be seen on the television, and that is where the world will watch this event unfold. These passages in Daniel are not minute detailed, yet the phrase "sit at the same table and lie to each other" is a micro statement. It is a conference table that is being referred to in this verse. The point of fulfilled prophecy is the ability to verify all the information given, yet there is nothing in historical records to indicate that this event ever occurred and historical records only give a brief outline of events, not a description such as two kings sitting at a table. This verse is in reference to the antichrist and the ruler of Egypt (whomever that might be) in a time in the future.

"The king of the north will return to his own country with great wealth, but his heart will be set against the holy covenant, He will take action against it and then return to his own country." (Daniel 11:28)

This verse immediately proceeds his visit with the ruler of Egypt, apparently he received his "great wealth" as a result of that meeting, yet it states that his heart is set against the holy covenant. The covenant again is the Abrahamic covenant in which the Israeli people are living in the land given to them by God according to the covenant God made with Abraham. This verse has nothing to do with the temple as of yet. It is simply the point where he breaks his agreement with the nation of Israel as "taking action against it". One can infer from both verses together that the antichrist had a meeting with the Egyptian leader and the outcome for the moment was favorable as the antichrist obtained wealth from it, apparently a discussion ensued at the meeting and part of the discussion was that the Egyptians are not pacified regarding his agreement with Israel; therefore he takes action against his original covenant confirmation with Israel immediately after he leaves Egypt but before he returns home. An historical point is that when Antiochus left Egypt, he did not leave with wealth, as he was defeated and he went immediately to Judea to slaughter the rebels. The massacre that occurred was not part of any agreement he made with Israel, they were merely rebelling Seleucid rule in their land. This meeting occurs before Egypt and the King of the North (the antichrist) go to war. The dialogue throughout this passage is chopped into sections that need to be pieced together. In Daniel 11:40 we find where the battle occurs, *"At the time of the end the king of the South will engage him in battle and the King of the North will storm out against him with chariots and cavalry and a great fleet of ships."* As we continue to dissect this passage two other verses match; Daniel 11:25-26 is part of this war and in verse 26 we find that the Egyptian ruler is being betrayed by his closest associates.

He will extend his power over many countries; Egypt will not escape. He will gain control of the treasures of gold and silver and all the riches of Egypt, with the Libyans and Nubians in submission. (Daniel 11:42-43)

The outcome of the battle is in favor of the antichrist. This verse confirms that he takes Egypt and other parts of Africa under his control; namely Libya and Sudan. The prophet Isaiah prophesied the same outcome in regards to Egypt during the last days:

I will stir up Egyptian against Egyptian-brother will fight against brother, neighbor against neighbor, city against city, kingdom against kingdom. The Egyptians will lose heart, and I will bring their plans to nothing; they will consult the idols and spirits of the dead, the mediums and the spiritists. I will hand the Egyptians over to the power of a cruel master and a fierce king will rule over them, declares the Lord, the Lord Almighty. The waters of the river will dry up and the riverbed will be parched and dry. The canals will stink; the streams of Egypt will dwindle and dry up. (Isaiah 19:2-6)

This is predicted of a time yet to come to Egypt, as the Nile has never dried up. The fierce king is one and the same as the stern faced king in Daniel, the antichrist. He shows contention with Egypt more than any other nation depicted in the bible; perhaps like the Hatfields and Mccoys, it is a centuries-old feud that he rekindles.

But reports from the east and the north will alarm him, and he will set out in a great rage to destroy and annihilate many. He will pitch his tents between the seas at the beautiful holy mountain. Yet he will come to his end, and no one will help him. (Daniel 11:44-45)

He will cause deceit to prosper, and he will consider himself superior. When they feel secure, he will destroy many and take his stand against the Prince of princes. Yet he will be destroyed, but not by human power. (Daniel 8:25)

This is the end of the eighth king. He is destroyed by Jesus when he returns as depicted in Revelation:

Then I saw the beast and the kings of the earth and their armies gathered to make war against the rider on the horse and his army. But the beast was captured, and with him the false prophet who had performed the miraculous signs on his behalf. With these signs he had deluded those who had received the mark of the beast and worshiped his image. The two of them were thrown alive into the fiery lake of burning sulfur. (Revelation 19:19-

It was you who broke the heads of the monster in the water. (Psalms 74:13)

The Foolish Shepherd

For false Christs and false prophets will appear

and perform great signs and miracles to

deceive even the elect- if that were possible.

— Matthew 24:24

Chapter 6

Part I

A Powerful Delusion

The coming of the lawless one will be in accordance with the work of Satan displayed in all kinds of counterfeit miracles, signs and wonders, and in every sort of evil that deceives those who are perishing. They perish because they refused to love the truth and so be saved. For this reason God sends them a powerful delusion so that they will believe the lie and so that all will be condemned who have not believed the truth but have delighted in wickedness. (2 Thessalonians 2: 9-12)

In Christian literature, the antichrist has stolen most of the spotlight during the tribulation; but there is another sinister villain to be found in the pages of the bible at the time of the end. He is called *"The False Prophet"*, and he will be responsible for thousands of deaths and deceiving the souls of mankind during the last days.

Because of the signs he was given power to do on behalf of the first beast, he deceived the inhabitants of the earth. (Revelation 13:14)

His coming was foretold by the prophet Zechariah and again in Revelation by the apostle John. He has many names, *"The false prophet, the foolish shepherd, the worthless shepherd, and the beast from the earth"*. Most Americans read the bible as an American; in other words, with a certain distance between yourself and the people in the bible and the nation of Israel. As an American born citizen, never having known famine or a war torn country, and living in a land of plenty for many generations it is sometimes difficult to understand the impact of the cataclysmic events in the prophetic books of the bible.

The events foretold in Revelation are of tremendous devastation all over the world. It is horrendous events, both natural and supernatural, occurring at the same time. In the natural realm, *"The earth dries up and withers, the earth's inhabitants are burned up, the earth is broken up and thoroughly shaken, and the earth reels like a drunkard"* (Isaiah 24:4-6,19-20); in the supernatural realm, *"fire mixed with blood and hail fall to the earth and one third of the vegetation dies, painful sores appear on followers of the beast, the sea is turned to blood and everything in it dies, one-third of the lakes and streams turn poisonous and the other two-thirds turn to blood leaving no potable water, demonic locusts are unleashed to torture those who follow the beast, and lastly, the sun moon and stars turn dark so there is no light."(Book of Revelation Chapters 6-19)*.

These events do not occur over a long period of time, but in a mere seven year period, and more so in the last three and a half years of this time period, which is referred to as the "Great Tribulation". Nations will be destroyed, never to rise again; continents will be devastated, some incapable of sustaining man or beast, and humans come close to near extinction levels. God says, *"I will make man scarcer than gold"* (Isaiah 13:12), and in Jesus' own words, *"If those days had not been cut short, no one would survive"* (Matthew 24:22). The inhabitants of the earth, those whose name is not written in the book of life, will wonder what is happening; more than likely the same ones who scoff at doomsday scenarios and Christian apocalyptic predictions. People will be looking for answers, and for someone who can lead them through this crisis of the planet; enter the False Prophet. Just as Batman had Robin, the Antichrist has a sidekick; and the Dragon bestows on him all the power he needs to deceive mankind. Satan knows that many people on earth are still awaiting their Messiah to come for the first time, therefore he gives almost unlimited supernatural power to this man called the False Prophet so he becomes believable or credible. The Jews and Muslims alike believe almost all of the stories of the Old Testament, including the return of Elijah as was discussed in a previous chapter; they are awaiting a forerunner to the Messiah, a prophet who can perform signs and miracles.

And he performed great and miraculous signs, even causing fire to come down from heaven to earth in full view of men. (Revelation 13:13)

That is the basis of Jesus's statement, *"A wicked and adulterous generation asks for a sign but none will be* given it except for the sign of Jonah" (Matthew 16:4); as Christians, we are not to look for someone performing signs and miracles, but to discern the truth through the spirit and prayer. Once he is believed to be the next Elijah, he can name the new Messiah, and he does. The False Prophet and the Antichrist have a symbiotic relationship; it is clear from scriptures that the false prophet adores and worships the Man of Sin, and the Antichrist in turn gives the False Prophet all of his acting powers as Supreme Ruler. In Revelation, it describes the decisions that are made by the False Prophet, acting on behalf of the Antichrist, which seem to be of unlimited power.

He exercised all the authority of the first beast on his behalf, and made the earth and its inhabitants worship the first beast, whose fatal wound had been healed. (Revelation 13:12)

Part II

The Third Temple

Then I saw another beast, coming out of the earth. He had two horns like a lamb, but he spoke like a dragon. (Revelation 13:11)

Here we see John giving the reader an allegorical description of the False Prophet; he is described as a beast coming out of the earth, which is polar opposite of the beast that came out of the sea. The "Sea" description, as we have already discussed, symbolizes many nations and people, in other words, the Gentile nations. The sea representing the Gentile nations is every ethnic group of people on earth besides the Jews; therefore the earth can only represent the nationality of people that are not Gentile, the Jewish nation.

He had two horns like a lamb, but he spoke like a dragon. (Revelation 13:11)

The representation of the "lamb" in this description gives the reader a clue to his ethnicity; Jesus is called "the lamb, and the lamb of God", but the lamb represents his nationality at birth. He is the first born of Israel, meaning of Jewish nationality, therefore the "lamb" in the above scripture also indicates that the False Prophet is of Jewish heritage, or a child of Israel.

Abraham was called out of the land of the Chaldeans in Ur, which is the ancient Mede/Persian Empire or modern Iraq. He was called out from the nation of the "ram" and God spoke him into another existence, thereby creating Abraham as the first and the father of the Jewish nation. The nation of Israel is always depicted as a woman or female, she gave birth to a lamb (Christ); which means that Abraham, when called out and separated by God, went from "ram" status to "sheep" status the moment God spoke it into existence. Jesus referred to the nation of Israel during his ministry as his "flock", and Jesus himself is depicted throughout scriptures as being the "Lamb of God"; a lamb was slain during the Israelites exodus from Egypt at Passover as representing a blood offering which would later become the role of the Messiah.

When God tested Abraham's faith, and asked him to sacrifice his son Isaac, he gave him a replacement to be slain as a sacrifice instead; that sacrifice was a ram. The sacrificed ram represented Ishmael and his descendants, as Ishmael and his mother were cast out of Abraham's tribe, because the promise of the covenant from God was bestowed on Abraham through Isaac only. The ram also represented Abraham in the natural world as a Chaldean in Ur before God called him out to be separate, whereas the covenant promise of Isaac was of supernatural origins. God had Abraham sacrifice his past in the natural world for an exchange of a friendship and relationship with God and the future promise; therefore the Jewish nation has always done the same in being separated from other nations; in exchange for being God's chosen people they had to sacrifice becoming one with the natural world in which the Gentiles lived. Whenever the nation of Israel has tried to bond with another nation, culture, or religion; they have come under bondage to that nation. They had become so enmeshed in Egyptian culture, that after the Exodus they grumbled about not having meat pots in the desert as they had in Egypt, they worshiped Babylonian and Assyrian gods and went into captivity under both empires, they became Hellenized under the Greeks and received brutal treatment from Antiochus Epiphanes, and they looked to Rome to crucify their Messiah resulting in their temple, city, and national identity being destroyed by Rome.

Some have missed the symbolism of this passage and used the verses in Revelation of the "lamb" beast depiction as an argument for it representing a Pope as the False Prophet. As we have already discussed previously, the Antichrist hates the prostitute and therefore would be unwilling to have a business relationship with her and grant her power, he will actually seek her destruction. The False Prophet will be of Jewish heritage; he will also be either a priest or the high priest in the new temple. He is referred to as a foolish shepherd, and a shepherd is only depicted in one aspect biblically; one who is in a position to shepherd the flock of Christ. He is portrayed by the prophet Zechariah as a replacement for Christ.

Zechariah 11:1-14 describes the first advent of Christ, and how he was treated by Israel as a nation.

So I pastured the flock marked for slaughter, particularly the oppressed of the flock. Then I took two staffs and called one Favor and the other Union and I pastured the flock. The flock detested me, and I grew weary of them and said, "I will not be your shepherd." (Zechariah 11:7-8)

Then he goes on to describe the breaking of the two staffs, and how God will raise up a shepherd over the land to replace Christ, whom was rejected.

Then the Lord said to me, "Take again the equipment of a foolish shepherd. For I am going to raise up a shepherd over the land who will not care for the lost, or seek the young, or heal the injured, or feed the healthy, but will eat the meat of the choice sheep tearing off their hoofs. (Zechariah 11:15-16)

This shepherd will be raised up over Israel in the last days, and will serve in the new temple that will be built there. He will eat his own flock; caring nothing for the nation of Israel, but only the power invested in him (first) by his position as Priest or High Priest, and (second) by the power granted to him by Satan. The nation of Israel has waited almost two millennia to rebuild a temple in Jerusalem; they will be completely enamored of an Israeli high priest serving in the temple for the first time in two thousand years, which will elevate him above suspicion to Jews and Christians when he is appointed to that position. Should Israel choose a priest by orthodox methods (and they will), then he will be a Levite as well. Christians, naturally, should support the nation of Israel, and they will support the Israelis building a new temple, however, many Christians have no idea of the ethnic origins of the false prophet and do not understand the ramifications of the new temple being built and the establishment of the high priest of that temple.

The Temple Institute in Israel has a website in which preparations and discussions are currently being made to someday rebuild the third Temple in Jerusalem. They have made many vessels for temple service already, and have recently completed the vestments for the high priest. The following is an excerpt from their website regarding the completion of the high priest vestments:

We are pleased to announce that the weaving of the sacred Ephod garment for the uniform of the High Priest has been completed. The Temple Institute has also completed the complicated task of joining the ephod to the remembrance stones, and affixing the breastplate.

This complex project has been based on extensive research by the Institute. With G-d's help this task has been completed and the results have been made public.

- The Temple Institute, Israel

The nation of Israel has had a temple as long as it has existed after establishing itself under King David. David wanted to build the temple for the Lord but because he had shed blood, God forbade him to do so, and told him that his son would build his house of worship. In Judea, life centered around the Temple, it defined the Jews as God's people; the Jews living without a Temple in Jerusalem is equivalent to an American living without a Constitution. One of the main reasons the temple has been stalled so long in being rebuilt is the secular Israeli government, in which they have forbade Jewish worship at Mount Moriah and turned over authority of the Temple Mount to the Muslims, so as not to unsettle international peace relations with other countries in regards to the Muslim shrine at the Dome of the Rock. The Muslims, taking advantage of that particular opportunity, have taken it one step further and insisted that no one at Mount Moriah is permitted to wear attire depicting Jewish or other religious symbols of their faith.

Part III

Executive Office of the High Priest

Looks can be deceiving; *"He had two horns like a lamb, but he spoke like a dragon"* (Revelation 13:11). He seems to be lacking in eloquence of speech; the phrasing of that scripture is comparing the speech of the False Prophet to Satanic rhetoric. With his new office will come not only unlimited power over Israel, but of all countries in which the Antichrist has jurisdiction; and with this newfound power comes the most heinous of crimes in all of history for he not only takes lives, but by deceiving the inhabitants of the earth, he is casting their soul into hell.

He ordered them to set up an image in honor of the beast who was wounded by the sword and yet lived. He was given power to give breath to the image of the first beast, so that it could speak and cause all who refused to worship the image to be killed.

(Revelation 13:14-15)

The only people on the planet that will refuse to worship the beast and accept martyrdom is Christians and possibly some Jews. All other people, regardless of their religion will accept the mark of the beast by loving their life more than their religious beliefs. Christians that face martyrdom will do so willingly as they will understand all of these prophecies and know

189

exactly what is happening. Some will also have a chance to testify before being beheaded. This is the abomination of desolation that was referred to by Daniel the prophet in Babylon in the year 586 BC and by Jesus himself during his earthly ministry. The abomination is two-fold in that the False Prophet, who is a Jewish High Priest, is recreating an act of God; as God breathed life into Adam made from dust, the False Prophet does the same to an "image" of the beast, and then there is the location of where this disgusting miscreation will be located. It is complete blasphemy in that the False Prophet has elevated himself to a "God" status by this blasphemous act. The Jewish temple has a room that is called the "Holy of Holies" and is located behind a curtain in which the ark of the covenant was kept and is also where God's spirit dwelt in Old Testament times; that is where this monstrosity is going to be placed, in the Holy of Holies where it will be referred to as the God of Israel. Only a Jewish High Priest and orthodox Jews will grasp the importance and full meaning of where this image is going to be located. When Antiochus Epiphanes sacrificed a pig on the Jewish altar and brought in an idol of Zeus into the Jewish temple, it was acts of blasphemies, but it was not an "abomination". The reader must understand that the Old Testament Jews were charged by God with the same behavior as they resorted to worshiping other gods in their temple as in the women "mourning Tammuz" in the outer court, but no one ever set up another idol inside the "Holy of Holies" nor did they ever "give breath or life" to an idol. That is the abomination; that is the unmistakable act that

190

prompts Jesus to give a specific warning to the people who live in Judea and witness this.

So when you see standing in the 'holy place' the abomination that causes desolation, spoken of through the prophet Daniel-let the reader understand- then let those who are in Judea flee to the mountains. Let no one on the roof of his house go down to take anything out of the house. Let no one in the field go back to get his cloak. How dreadful it will be in those days, for pregnant women and nursing mothers! Pray that your flight will not take place in winter or on the Sabbath. For then there will be great distress, unequaled from the beginning of the world until now and never to be equaled again. (Matthew 24:15-21)

Jesus is saying when the Israelis witness this specific event, to get out of town, leave the inhabited areas of Israel and run to the mountains of either northern Israel or cross the border into the mountainous desert regions and seek safety. Many biblical expositors have placed the refugees as fleeing to Petra as it is carved into the mountains, but Jesus was not specific, only a dire warning to leave Judea. It is the aftermath of that abominable act that the False Prophet begins his murderous campaign, as he will realize that there will be many dissenters trying to escape Israel; that is another reason Jesus states to not go back to your home and pack your bags, not even to get a coat. The Middle Eastern world will be policed by the forces of the Antichrist and anyone seen trying to pack to leave would either be caught and arrested or shot. These events take us to the next order of business of the Executive Office of the High Priest.

Codes – The Mark of the Beast

Throughout the book of Revelation, there is a theme of those taking the "mark of the beast", and the martyred souls who choose not to follow the beast and are triumphant. The mark is originated from none other than the False Prophet.

He also forced everyone, small and great, rich and poor, free and slave to receive a mark on his right hand or on his forehead, so that no one could buy or sell unless he had the mark which is the name of the beast, or the number of his name. (Revelation 13:16)

Though the mark pertains to the Antichrist, it is the invention of the False Prophet to label everyone as livestock or "property of" the Beast. 'Buying' is anything from food supplies to gas for your vehicle and could even mean utilities for your home; 'selling' is goods or services provided by an individual and are paid for by a merchant or an employer, meaning the ability of obtaining or keeping employment.

The Mark

There are many different ideas floating around on the internet about what the "mark" is; anything from a biochip implant, a barcode, or a tattoo. My opinion is, it doesn't matter; that is not being said in callousness, but the only thing that matters at that point is whether you receive it or not. It will not secretly be done to a person, every individual on the planet will have a choice and it will be clear that to take this mark means you are choosing the antichrist-they will not try to dupe you by telling you it is a vaccination; and I'm sure someone is not going to decline it because it is a biochip implant instead of a barcode. The technology is already there for any number of ways to track a person or keep up with their spending and employment; the technology should not be the scarier concept, it is much like a weapon, the power given to an individual to use it against mankind. To accept or not accept the mark is a life or death decision physically and spiritually; to accept it would mean to gain your physical life momentarily and lose your life in the spiritual sense for all eternity.

All inhabitants of the earth will worship the beast-all whose names have not been written in the book of life belonging to the lamb that was slain from the creation of the world. (Revelation 13:8)

They perish because they refused to love the truth and so be saved. (2 Thessalonians 2:10)

To deny the mark could mean to lose your physical life either immediately by being martyred and gain eternal salvation which would begin the moment you are martyred, or at a later time by such factors as starvation or exposure and gain eternal salvation at the return of Jesus.

Therefore put on the full armor of God, so that when the day of evil comes, you may be able to stand your ground and after you have done everything, to stand. (Ephesians 6:13)

Consider it pure joy, my brothers, whenever you face trials of many kinds, because you know that the testing of your faith develops perseverance. (James 1:2-3)

You need to persevere so that when you have done the will of God, you will receive what he has promised. For in just a very little while, He who is coming will come and will not delay. But my righteous one will live by faith. And if he shrinks back, I will not be pleased with him. But we are not of those who shrink back and are destroyed, but of those who believe and are saved. (Hebrews 10:36-39)

The hype surrounding the speculation on what the mark actually will be should not be the issue for Christians, for these speculations diverts one's attention away from the most important issue. The question is, would you accept or deny the mark of the beast?

For whoever wants to save his life will lose it, but whoever loses his life for me will save it. What good is it for a man to gain the whole world and yet lose or forfeit his very self? (Luke 9:24)

The Meaning of the Mark

The particular scripture about the mark of the beast has baffled scholars, clergy and laymen for millennia. It is the most speculated upon and probably the most widely known scripture in the entire bible. Multiple translations are:

This calls for wisdom. If anyone has insight, let him calculate the number of the beast, for it is man's number. His number is 666. (Revelation 13:18)- NIV (1984)

Wisdom is needed here Let the one with understanding solve the meaning of the number of the beast, for it is the number of a man. His number is 666. (Revelation 13:18) NLT (2007)

In this situation wisdom is needed. Let the person who has insight figure out the number of the beast, because it is a human number. The beast's number is 666.   (Revelation 13:18)
God's Word Translation (1995)

The bible is God's words to mankind spoken through his prophets, it is also a puzzle or a mystery and one of the main reasons why Jesus spoke in parables is not for the casual reader, but to study the word of God and petition God for revelation; a verse from the Old Testament can have its meaning translated from a verse in the New Testament and vice versa. Using a verse from scripture, one can almost use the entire bible to back it up and usually should be done in this manner so as to not take scripture out of its intended context.

In the verse from Revelation 13:18, wisdom equals insight and could be interchangeable as it is phrased.

Definition of **Insight:**

1. The capacity to discern the true nature of a situation

2. The act or outcome of grasping the hidden nature of things or perceiving in an intuitive manner
3. The immediate understanding of the significance of an event

Many people, when reading this scripture become focused on the number and view it as a mathematical problem, whereas it cannot be a math problem as there is no problem, only an answer in the sum of 666, six hundred and sixty six, or six hundred three score and six. Regardless of how it is written, it is the same number. Another bizarre method some have used is to try to substitute letters for numbers of various modern and ancient alphabets of Hebrew, Greek, Latin or even English to come up with many different personages; ancient and modern, including Prince Charles of Wales and, of course, the pope using the words, "Vicarious Filii Dei". The constant "grasping at straws" by Christians claiming to have the answer to something sensational is proof that it did not come through intense biblical study or logic; it is almost the equivalent to date setting. One point to remember, the first advent of Jesus is the most prophesied event in the Old Testament, yet he was never named in prophecy, only the quality of his character was given, *"And he shall be called Wonderful Counselor, Mighty God, Everlasting Father and Prince of peace."*(Isaiah 9:6)

The irony of the situation is, if a Jewish Hebrew scholar believed in the New Testament and would read the book of Revelation, he would know what this phrase was in reference to; however, this scripture in the New Testament that has such a huge impact on Israel happens to be from a book that orthodox Jews don't believe is relevant to Judaism.

John wrote the book of Revelation while he was exiled on the isle of Patmos awaiting a Roman execution. He received his visions from Jesus himself, and his only source of reference beyond the words of Jesus was the Old Testament, as he had not even perused any of the New Testament because it had not been compiled into a single bible, but many different letters from many different apostles. The book of Revelation exists today because John wrote it in code; should a Roman guard come into his room and inspect the material he was laboring on, it would have seemed like unimportant "religious" material or nonsense. He also had the important task of keeping the new churches that were mostly composed of Jewish converts safe from orthodox Jews and Romans that did not hesitate to execute those who were of the new faith. John wrote Revelation in 95 AD, twenty five years after the second temple had been destroyed, and an apostle that had studied the Old Testament would have known from many different prophetic books in the Old Testament that a new Temple would someday be built in Jerusalem and that it confirmed his vision. He also knew that God's word is the only thing guaranteed to endure for two millennia as a source of reference. Revelation 13:18 is a word problem or a word puzzle; paraphrased, the verse according to the definition of insight would read:

"This calls for wisdom, if anyone has the immediate understanding of the significance of an event, let him figure out what the number of the beast means, for it is in reference to a man, his number is 666."

The two questions that come from that verse would be (first) which man? and (second) what significant event?

His source of reference can be found in 1 Kings 10:14:

> *The weight of the gold that Solomon received yearly was 666 talents*

It is not about the number 666 in itself, it is a reference in the direction of King Solomon; the number 666 is not found anywhere else in scripture. Secondly, it is not about King Solomon specifically, but what King Solomon is remembered for; wealth, wisdom, and building the first Jewish Temple in Israel. This number specifically points to his wealth that made building King Solomon's Temple possible. The Jews had established the nation of Israel under King David, but they did not have a temple, only a tent to house the Ark of the Covenant. The very first temple ever built in Israel was constructed by King Solomon; he was the wealthiest man in the world in his time, and his temple was the most splendid, the interior of it was overlaid with gold. What he is remembered for is building the first Jewish Temple, and what John wanted readers to understand is, the *"significance of building a new Jewish Temple in Israel"*. It is the crucial moment when these events begin to happen. The Jewish people were completely displaced from 135

AD until 1948 AD for a total of 1813 years; why would the Jews wait nearly seventy years, as of now, in their homeland without pushing for a new temple to be built? The reason is God's timing, with the new temple comes the time of the end. An article from an online Israeli newspaper stated that the Israeli Jews seem somewhat lethargic about building a new temple, except for a few pockets of protest, it is as if the Jewish nation as a whole does not really care if they have a temple built or not. That is God's power over Israel now, the majority of the population does not care about a temple being built again; but they will care in the future. God will eliminate the lethargy from their minds and a consuming desire will come upon the nation of Israel to have a third temple built in Jerusalem. When reading the prophetic books of the Old Testament, and especially Ezekiel, one realizes how many of the prophecies have come to pass already with the Jews as a nation returning to their homeland. Following the natural logical thought process, with the historical data regarding the nation of Israel, the bible reader should realize that the Jews have always had a temple in Jerusalem, or had been in the process of building one.

The mark itself has even been misinterpreted, *"The mark, which is the name of the beast or the number of his name"*; such as the iron cross in Germany represented the Nazis, it was a symbol. The mark will be a symbol for the name of the beast and his conglomeration of power, including both the secular and religious aspects. Since the number of the beast represents the Jewish Temple and the name of the beast is the name of the Antichrist; then it is one mark that represents both the Antichrist and the False Prophet.

AWOL

Woe to the worthless shepherd, who deserts the flock! May the sword strike his arm and his right eye! May his arm be completely withered, his right eye totally blinded! (Zechariah 11:17)

In the last days, Israel is invaded and those who did not flee to the mountains as Jesus advised will be left in Jerusalem. The False Prophet not only turns their hearts away from worshiping the true God but will actually desert them when the environment in Jerusalem becomes violent beyond his control. The scriptures in Zechariah that describe the False Prophet state the "*sword will strike his arm and his right eye*"; the sword is in reference to an act of war which could be during an invasion that occurs in Israel in the last days, the people who do not leave are his actual followers yet he deserts them.'

"Awake, O sword, against my shepherd, against the man who is close to me!" declares the Lord Almighty. Strike the shepherd, and the sheep will be scattered and I will turn my hand against the little ones. (Zechariah 13:7)

The reference to "*the one who is close to me*" is the act of temple service in that priests come close to the Lord as described in Leviticus. This act of striking the shepherd breaks the hold of his followers, and they are left with no one to look to when Israel is invaded. The Lord says he will turn his hands against the little ones,

200

meaning the deluded flock that has followed the False Prophet.

In the whole land, declares the Lord, two-thirds will be struck down and perish; yet one-third will be left in it. This third I will bring into the fire; I will refine them like silver and test them like gold. They will call on my name and I will answer them. I will say, they are my people and they will say, The lord is our God. (Zechariah 13:8-9)

God brings one-third of the Jewish nation through this and refines them. This verse matches the verses found in Daniel.

Those who are wise will instruct many, though for a time they will fall by the sword or be burned or captured or plundered. When they fall they will receive a little help, and many who are not sincere will join them. Some of the wise will stumble, so that they may be refined, purified and made spotless until the time of the end. For it will still come at the appointed time. (Daniel 11:33-35)

The appointed time is the return of Christ; at his return the Jewish nation will recognize him as their Messiah.

They will look on me, the one they have pierced, and they will mourn for him, as one mourns for an only child, and grieve bitterly for him as one grieves for a firstborn son. On that day the weeping in Jerusalem will be great like the weeping of Hadad Rimmon in the plain of Megiddo. (Zechariah 12:10-11)

At the second advent of Christ, he will put his enemies under his feet.

But the beast was captured; and with him the false prophet who had performed the miraculous signs on his behalf. With these signs he had deluded those who had received the mark of the beast and worshiped his image. The two of them were thrown alive into the fiery lake of burning sulfur. (Revelation 19:20)

The end of a very short career of the False Prophet will occur at the return of Messiah.

Lifespan of a King

The length of our days is seventy years-

or eighty, if we have the strength; yet their

span is but trouble and sorrow, for they quickly

pass, and we fly away. — Psalms 90:10

Chapter 7

The End from the Beginning

At that time Tyre will be forgotten for seventy years, the span of a king's life. (Isaiah 23:15)

The Jews established their nation by conquering Canaan under leaders such as Joshua, and then the Lord gave them Judges; but the Israelites complained that all the other nations around them had kings as their leaders, and they also wanted a king to rule over them. The first king God anointed for Israel was Saul, who did not keep the commands of God, so God looked for a replacement for him. On a battlefield, facing a giant, a small shepherd took a slingshot and felled Goliath; the Jews saw their new king in action, but the position came with risks. The spirit of God left Saul, and he basically turned into a madman; he pursued the newly anointed king named David until his death. When David finally took his throne, the nation of Israel still had many problems, it was unsettled and wars were constantly being fought with the peoples who were either not killed initially or driven out of Canaan when they first took possession of the land. David's career was spent fighting against enemies of Israel; he was anointed by God as king and was also a warrior. He yearned to build a house for God, but the Lord refused him.

The verse from Isaiah of the span of a king's life was in reference to King David; the Lord called him a man after his own heart, and his covenant with David was that he would have a house and one from his family on the throne in Israel forever. He is the most revered king Israel ever had, with the exception of the Messiah to Christians, and the span of a king's life was in comparison to King David, as he lived seventy years.

Remember the former things, those of long ago; I am God and there is no other, I am God, and there is none like me. I make known the end from the beginning, from ancient times, what is still to come. (Isaiah 46:9-10)

The Jewish nation has come full circle from being established as a nation to their exile in 135 AD and their return to Israel again in 1948. It is their return to Israel that marked the beginning of being re-established as a nation again, and like under King David, that establishment has come with many wars and enemies on every side that feel Israel does not have a right to exist as a nation in their promised land. The Jews were exiled to Babylon for seventy years, and upon their return to Judea, they commenced building the second temple. The first temple built in Jerusalem was constructed by King Solomon when he took the throne after his father David. The lifespan of King David is directly connected to David's covenant with God in that David would always have one from his line on the throne of Israel. That covenant was never abolished; its result was the manifestation of the Messiah that will establish his earthly kingdom during his millennial reign. The throne is legally the

Messiah's, but the earthly covenant with King David has resulted in the Jews being "stuck" in the cycle of "seventy" because of their initial rejection of the Messiah. The Jews were exiled to Babylon for seventy years, they were given seventy weeks of years in Daniel's prophecy, and the Jews have been in their homeland for nearly seventy years since returning. The numbers seven and seventy are numbers, when pertaining to the Jews, of restoration and completion; their country was restored and their temple was finally built under King Solomon after seventy years under King David's reign. The Jews are once again in the cycle of seventy years of restoration in Israel, they needed time to re-establish their nation, and for the majority of the Jewish population to return home; to put it bluntly, it has not been the time for them to rebuild their temple. As King Solomon built the first temple after his father's seventy year reign, the Jews will build their temple after the seventy year completion of restoration since returning to their homeland. When after the seventy years? That answer is unknown as God does not use a manmade calendar, but King Solomon only reigned fifty odd years; that is the historic cycle of Jewish history, and the reason the Jews have had to wait this long before building their third temple.

Holy Real Estate

The Lord said to Abram after Lot had parted from him, "Lift up your eyes from where you are and look north and south, east and west. All the land that you see I will give to you and your offspring forever. (Genesis 13:14-15)

The reconstruction of the third temple has issues now that were not present during the construction of the first and second temples, namely the Dome of the Rock and the Al-Aqsa Mosque belonging to the Muslim faith that sits atop the Temple Mount in Jerusalem. It is the most contested piece of real estate on the globe. The Israelis, under the Abrahamic Covenant, have a claim to the entire state of Israel, yet the Arabs argue that the Israelis have no claim to the Temple Mount or any other part of Israel and that they are merely occupying Arab land. Then there is the fairly new issue of where the first two temples actually stood; in the last 30 years, many different archaeologists and professors have contested that the traditional location of the Temple Mount might not be the original one. There are two other locations that some believe could have been the original site of the first and second temples, their theories of locations are based upon archaeological excavations, extensive documentation and research. The disputed locations are the northern conjuncture supported by Physicist Asher Kaufman, which is north of the Dome of the Rock, and the southern conjuncture supported by Tel Aviv architect Tuvia Sagiv, being south of the Dome of the Rock, in addition to the traditional site atop the Temple Mount directly where the Dome of the Rock currently resides.

The state of Israel will not build a third temple until the exact location of the previous two temples are ascertained; at this time they are unable to perform archaeological excavations at the Temple Mount as it is now under Muslim control. There are many dynamics involved with regards to the Temple Mount that could result in a Jewish Temple being built, yet it would be a pointless endeavor in speculation. That is a semi-secular point of view as to the current situation of Jerusalem and the Temple Mount; however, there is another opinion, a biblical one...

Ezekiel's Temple

I am the Lord your God, who brought you out of Egypt, out of the land of slavery. You shall have no other gods before Me. (Exodus 20:2-3)

Israel had an opportunity to take the Temple Mount, along with the old city of Jerusalem in the 6 Day War in 1967; they didn't, however, from fear of repercussions from allied nations such as the US. They allowed the Temple Mount, the Most Holy place in Israel and the world, to remain occupied by Muslims when they could have had control of what is rightfully theirs in fellowship and covenant with God.

I, even I, am he who comforts you. Who are you that you fear mortal men, the sons of men, who are but grass, that you forget the Lord your Maker, who stretched out the heavens and laid the foundations of the earth, that you live in constant terror every day because of the wrath of the oppressor who is bent on destruction? For where is the wrath of the oppressor? (Isaiah 51:12-13)

Since opting out of that opportunity, the Israelis have had to return large portions of land won during the Six Day War back to the Arab nations, with constant pressure to give more. What good is the land God promised Israel without the God that promised it? The book of Ezekiel describes the situation on the Temple Mount and the conditions before the third temple is *built.*

When they placed their threshold next to my threshold and their doorposts beside my doorposts, with only a wall between me and them they defiled my holy name by their detestable practices. (Ezekiel 43:8)

The Israelites left Judea in 135 AD, after 1813 years they returned home, only to find their house occupied by strangers. Instead of ousting the home invaders, they set up their home beside the one they already had and let the invaders stay. They stand at a wall and wail for the home that is rightfully theirs, *only a wall that separates them from their covenant with God.* The last seven chapters of Ezekiel deal with a future time in Israel, and specifically the millennial temple; therefore the words of God spoken in Ezekiel are of the same time frame. The prophecy teachers of the main media outlets have failed to see that Israel has had to give up land because she did not fulfill her covenant with God. They captured the old city of Jerusalem only to be able to stand outside of their Temple Mount to pray; their first priority should have been the Temple Mount and the God of Israel.

The verses continue with a monologue from God stating that if Israel is ashamed of her sins, consider the plans of the new temple and build it. The end of the monologue is the current situation of the Temple Mount and God is firm in that it cannot be shared by other religions, and other peoples.

This is the law of the temple: All the surrounding area on top of the mountain will be most holy. Such is the law of the temple. (Ezekiel 43:12)

At this point God has chastised Israel and especially the secular government for giving control of the Temple Mount to the Arabs; however, the Temple has not been built, as God tells them if they are ashamed of their sins, *then* consider the plans of the temple. Then we come to a peculiar verse; it is spoken by God in a future time before the third temple is built.

In addition to all your other detestable practices, you brought foreigners uncircumcised in heart and flesh into my sanctuary, desecrating my temple while you offered me food, fat and blood, and you broke my covenant. (Ezekiel 44:7)

Again, this goes back to the former law of the temple, that the Temple Mount cannot be shared. The foreigners uncircumcised in heart and flesh are the Muslims on the Temple Mount. These verses combined together give the reader a picture of what will happen in the future; the Jews will at some point share the Temple Mount with the Muslims, and before building the temple; they will build an altar and offer sacrifices. We know as of now the Israelis do not perform sacrifices; yet, the book of Ezra lays the foundation for the commencement of building the temple when the Jews returned from Babylon.

Then Jeshua son of Jozadak and his fellow priests and Zerubbabel son of Shealtiel and his associates began to build the altar of the God of Israel to sacrifice burnt offerings on it, in accordance with what is written in the Law of Moses the man of God. Despite their

fear of the peoples around them they built the altar on its
foundation and sacrificed burnt offerings on it to the Lord both the
morning and evening sacrifices. (Ezra 3:2-3)

On the first day of the seventh month they began to offer burnt
offerings to the Lord, though the foundation of the Lord's temple
had not been laid. (Ezra 3:6)

The fact that at some point in the future the Jewish people agree to share the Temple Mount with the Muslims for religious purposes is a testament that although they are Jewish and living in the promised land, they do not understand their God in the way that their ancestors did. They will take the modern politically correct road to try and appease the United Nations. Judaism is the oldest active religion in the world, with the exception of some far eastern religions; and the Arabs, who say that the Temple Mount has always belonged to them, testify against themselves in the Quran when they acknowledge Abraham as their father, along with many other prophets of the Old Testament. The Lord continues in his chastisement;

Instead of carrying out your duty in regard to my holy things, you
put others in charge of my sanctuary. This is what the sovereign
Lord says: no foreigner uncircumcised in heart and flesh is to enter
my sanctuary, not even the foreigners who live among the
Israelites. (Ezra 44:8-9)

The modern Jewish people have not had a Temple to worship at for almost 2,000 years; they are far removed from the customs of the ancient Temple. Religious orthodox Jews have had to study the scriptures and learn the customs again and they have established The Temple Institute, which is crafting the temple objects for service; but these items are being put on display and some have been sent to museums for anybody to gawk at. The Jews have forgotten what "Holy" means, that it is not for secular display, but for a worship service to a "Holy God". They are like fish out of water in regards to their temple. The uniform of the High Priest that has been completed by The Temple Institute is displayed on their website, yet in Ezekiel, it states of the priests who are to serve in the temple,

When they go out into the outer court where the people are, they are to take off the clothes they have been ministering in and are to leave them in the sacred rooms, and put on other clothes, so that they do not consecrate the people by means of their garments. (Ezekiel 44:19)

An Old Testament lesson about the Holy things of a Holy God; when Moses was instructing the new priesthood, Aaron and his sons, two of his sons offered unauthorized fire to the Lord, and they were consumed with fire that came from God.

Among those who approach me I will show myself holy; in the sight of all the people I will be honored. (Leviticus 10:3)

Should the Jews choose at some point to share the Temple Mount with the Muslim shrines there by building an altar to make sacrifices, it will be a disaster for those involved. When God said "*so I destroyed them in my anger*", he was referring to those who perform this ceremony, not the entire nation of Israel. The nation of Israel has received many blessings from God since establishing their country, and will receive many more, if they do not succumb to international pressure, for with every compromise; they lose more of their inheritance.

A Great Horde

Ezekiel's temple will be built before Christ's return, as the plans are laid out for the people to build it and the same sacrifices are to be offered, which will not occur after Christ returns. This is a future prophecy in Ezekiel that follows on the heels of a multi-Arabic Muslim coalition that tries to converge on Israel. This confederation includes Tubal, Meshech, Gomer, and Togarmah; all of which are located in what is now modern Turkey, along with Persia, Put and Cush which are the modern countries of Iraq, Libya, and Ethiopia. The entire armies of invaders are killed on the mountains of northern Israel by a supernatural event, of which God says *"And I will show my greatness and my holiness, and I will make myself known in the sight of many nations. Then they will know that I am the Lord." – Ezekiel 38:23*

Some believe this event is the battle of Armageddon; this is an incorrect interpretation of scriptures, as the last days of Israel will not be in peace and culminates with the Jewish nation fleeing to the mountains for safety. It states in Ezekiel that these nations notice that Israel is living in peace and safety.

On that day thoughts will come into your mind and you will devise an evil scheme. You will say, "I will invade a land of unwalled villages, I will attack a peaceful and unsuspecting people-all of them living without walls and without gates and bars.
(Ezekiel 38:10-11)

In that day, when my people Israel are living in safety, will you not take notice of it? You will come from your place in the far north, you and many nations with you all of them riding on horses a great horde, a mighty army. You will advance against my people Israel like a cloud that covers the land. (Ezekiel 38:14-16)

At this point, we have many factors that must occur before the third temple in Israel will be built; If the timeline of Ezekiel is told chronologically, then a Muslim invasion against Israel will be launched in the future without success. The invaders will die on the mountains of Israel. Following this invasion, we have the description of the third temple to be built, once they have decided for certain that the original location of the temple is the actual temple site, they will somehow gain approval to resume sacrifices as is the custom of the temple before it is built. The open show of power from God could be the catalyst that spurs the Jews into rebuilding the temple. It will of course be shared with the Muslims on the Temple Mount, which will culminate with those involved in the sacrifices being destroyed by God as a reminder that God and the Temple Mount are still as holy today as He was 2,000 years ago.

This is the reason for prophecy, so that as Christians, we know what was foretold by the prophets is to happen before the apocalypse begins. Unfortunately, we have the rapture group that are in denial of scriptural teachings, and other Christian segments, that instead of following the line of prophecy in order, feel like the world could be destroyed at any time thereby spreading panic based on sensationalism. Prophecy can bring order to chaos, however, prophecy misused can stir sects into a frenzy that has resulted in cult-like behavior to the point of selling all their possessions and quitting their jobs because they know for certain which day Christ will return or, at the very worst, committing suicide.

The scriptures are very clear on what Christians are to be doing up until the time of the real end:

(First) Use the talents God gave each individual for the kingdom of God while you are here as Jesus spoke of in the parable of the talents (Matthew 25:14-30)

*(Second) Those who are able, earn your living and do not rely on the government
(1 Timothy 5:13, 2 Thessalonians 3:6, 11-12, 1 Thessalonians 4:11, Proverbs 18:9, 20:4)*

(Third) Obey the gospel, share the gospel, do what is instructed in the gospel   (2 Timothy 3:16, 2 Thessalonians 1:8, Mark 16:15, James 1:22-25)

(Fourth) Watch, as described as a "watchman on the wall" for the signs of the times of the end (Jesus describes watching for his return in the parable of the 10 virgins in Matthew 25:1-13, and other verses

imploring Christians to watch and be aware of the times, Luke 21:34-36, Matthew 24:42, Ezekiel 3:17)

The most dangerous concept of the pre-tribulation rapture is that it leads Christians to believe that there is nothing to worry about, that Jesus will return before the apocalyptic scenario begins. There will be many disillusioned Christians when they realize that they have believed a lie.

For the time will come when men will not put up with sound doctrine. Instead, to gather around them a great number of teachers to say what their itching ears want to hear. They will turn their ears away from the truth and turn aside to myths. (2 Timothy 4:3-4)

You boast, "We have entered into a covenant with death, with the grave we have made an agreement. When an overwhelming scourge sweeps by, it cannot touch us, <u>for we have made a lie our refuge and falsehood our hiding place.</u> (Isaiah 28:15)

The worst possible outcome would be that some Christians, believing that Christ returns first, will believe the False Prophet and be deceived. Jesus warned that false prophets would emerge, and they began to emerge in the mid 1800's; many new "Christian" religions were established during that time, and many of them were based on the testimony of false prophets such as Joseph Smith and the establishment of the Mormon Church, and Ellen G. White which began the Seventh Day Adventists. No church should ever be formed or centered based on a prophet or their message. These churches glorify the "prophets" as much or more than the God of the bible, and a cyclic pattern of these churches are that they eventually reject the original doctrine of the bible with a new form of doctrine coughed up by their "prophet" and what God "revealed" to them. Any prophet that does not come preaching in the name of Jesus Christ and not holding to the original doctrine of the bible as put forth by Jesus himself, and the apostles that followed is a false prophet. We see the final false prophet in action, deceiving thousands and possibly millions during Daniel's seventieth week.

Daniel's 70th Week

"Watchman, what is left of the night?

"Watchman, what is left of the night?

The watchman replies,

"Morning is coming, but also the night"

Isaiah 21:11-12

✛

Chapter 8

Seventy "Sevens"

Seventy 'sevens' are decreed for your people and your holy city to finish transgression, to put an end to sin, to atone for wickedness, to bring in everlasting righteousness, to seal up vision and prophecy and to anoint the most holy. (Daniel 9:24)

Daniel was petitioning God in prayer and praying for atonement for the sins of his people when the angel, Gabriel, appeared before him. He told him that the moment he began to pray an answer was given from the Lord and that he would explain what would happen to his people, the Israelites, after they were released from captivity of Babylon. Gabriel begins his narrative by telling Daniel that a total of seventy 'sevens' are the cumulative number of "weeks" for his people, meaning the Jews. This narrative is in a form of a mathematical word problem; the weeks, as described here are weeks of years; seven days in a week multiplied by the number seventy is 490 years total. The angel then tells Daniel of the starting point, and ending point for all but one of these weeks to be completed.

Know and understand this: from the issuing of the decree to restore and rebuild Jerusalem until the Anointed one comes, there will be seven 'sevens', and sixty –two 'sevens'. It will be rebuilt with streets and a trench, but in times of trouble. After the sixty-two 'sevens', the Anointed One will be cut off and will have nothing. (Daniel 9:25-26)

The judgment was brought about while the Jews were in captivity in Babylon for a total of seventy years. The Jews had failed to observe the sabbatical year for many years, in which the land was to lie fallow or at rest, and not be harvested, and also in which slaves were given the opportunity to be freed from their masters as well as all debts were canceled. The same concept is used on our modern credit reports in which bad debts after seven years are erased from the report.

The issuing of the decree to restore and rebuild Jerusalem is found in Nehemiah chapter 2, under King Artaxerxes in the month of Nisan in the twentieth year of his reign, Nehemiah makes his request to the king to return to Jerusalem and rebuild it. The king grants his request, and the building of Jerusalem's walls commenced, but amongst opposition from many different sides, from the Jews themselves who had mortgaged their fields to rebuild it, and from their enemies.

Meanwhile, the people in Judah said, "The strength of the laborers is giving out, and there is so much rubble that we cannot rebuild the wall." Also our enemies said, "Before they know it or see us, we will be right there among them and will kill them and put an end to the work." (Nehemiah 4:10-11)

So it occurred exactly as described by the angel, they were opposed while building the walls of Jerusalem.

The angel specified the decree was for the rebuilding of Jerusalem, not just the temple. The first decree that was issued from Cyrus the Persian was to rebuild the temple; the second decree was from King Artaxerxes to rebuild Jerusalem.

Adding the weeks of seven 'sevens' and sixty-two 'sevens' gives a total of sixty-nine weeks from the issuing of the decree in 445 BC until Jesus, the Anointed One, comes or began his ministry, with a total of 483 biblical years (476 solar/lunar years) fulfilled historically. His ministry began in 31 AD (he was thirty years old) and continued for three and a half years (the sign of Jonah again), he was crucified, or cut off, in 34 AD (after the sixty-two sevens) and the temple was destroyed in 70 AD; afterwards, the Jews were dispersed into the nations in 135 AD under the Emperor Hadrian, when he destroyed Jerusalem. The Gospel of Christ, which the Jews rejected, spread through Christianity; this period which has endured several millennia has become known as the 'Church Age', and is also referred to biblically as the 'times of the gentiles'; *"Jerusalem will be trampled on by the Gentiles until the times of the Gentiles are fulfilled"* – *Luke 21:24*

Jesus gave that message during his "Apocalyptic Discourse", and followed by giving other signs of his return at the end of the tribulation, therefore the reader can come to the conclusion that the 'times of the gentiles' will continue until the return of Christ the Messiah in his second advent. Some bible expositors do not give credence to the "gap theory", which is an intermission of an undisclosed number of years between the destruction of Jerusalem and the return of Christ; however, the testimony of Jesus in Luke 21:24, validates this as truth. The Jews, who rejected the Messiah in 34 AD, could not continue with their 'seventy weeks of years', as the entire reason the seventy weeks were given was hinged on the return of the Messiah, and the gospel of Christ being spread throughout the nations. The Jews rejected the New Testament message; therefore, the clock had to be stopped for the spread of Christianity. Some preterist expositors have stated that the entire dialogue between Gabriel and Daniel was fulfilled in entirety with the first advent of the Messiah; since the rebirth of Israel in 1948, this can no longer be considered even remotely valid in scriptures, as it only serves the purpose of 'replacement theology' in that the Church has replaced the Jews as God's chosen people. Throughout history, as long as the Jews were not in the land God promised them, some segments of the church held that the Jews, since rejecting Christ, were no longer a chosen people of God. Since their return in 1948, and with the un-doubtable blessings God has shown them since then, it is irrefutable that God has never broken his covenant with them, but has instead, fulfilled his very words to them:

Remember the instruction you gave your servant Moses, saying "If you are unfaithful, I will scatter you among the nations, but if you return to me and obey my command, then even if your exiled people are at the farthest horizon, I will gather them from there and bring them to the place I have chosen as a dwelling for my name." (Nehemiah 1:8-9)

As a Christian, we are grafted into the family of God, meaning the Jewish people who are the "parent" of Christianity, therefore these blessings and curses apply to us as well. It would behoove every Christian to at least read through the Old Testament, for when you stray from God's covenant in your own personal life, God employs discipline and there is usually a reason to be found in the Old Testament. "Grafting" as applied in this context, is botanical; and when another species of plant life is grafted into a "vine" it takes on the characteristics of the vine itself, the vine does not change to accommodate the new plant. Christianity is not a new or different religion than Judaism in a religious context, only in that as a Christian, one fulfills the written Old Testament prophecies regarding Christ in believing that he replaced the need for ritual temple sacrifice, whereas the Jews did not accept or believe that message; therefore we became part of the family of God. When a Christian comes to Christ, it is the same concept of the Israelites in Egypt spreading blood on their doorposts, in that a Christian is covered by the blood of the lamb. He did not throw out the old family and acquire a new one. That concept is verified in the New Testament when we are referred to as sons and co-heirs with Christ.

There is most assuredly a gap of twenty centuries and still counting from the sixty-ninth week to the seventieth week. The Messiah was "cut off" when he was 33 years old; some expositors believe that Jesus was born prior to the year that changed everything from BC to AD. With the exception that there was no year 0 AD, which places the birth of Christ in 1 AD, he

225

was born according to prophecy and exact calendar years of Daniel's Seventy weeks prophecy. There are two important scriptures that prove this:

"Do you see all these things?" He asked. "I tell you, not one stone here will be left on another; every one will be thrown down" (Matthew 24:2)

After the sixty-two sevens, the anointed one will be cut off and will have nothing.(Daniel 9:26)

The destruction of the temple was symbolic of Christ's crucifixion but it did not occur when Christ was crucified, it happened in 70 AD which was 69 real time years from the birth of Christ in 1 AD (symbolically 69 weeks of years). After the sixty-two weeks, the Messiah was cut off, because that was the end of the sixty-nine weeks of years prophecy and it states "the anointed one was cut off *and would have nothing*"; after Jesus was crucified the Jewish nation still went to the temple; when the temple was destroyed as symbolic of Christ's physical body he literally had no connection to the nation of Israel or 'had nothing'. As was discussed in the chapter 'Lifespan of a King', Jesus should have lived seventy years, but his life was cut short (in half) of the seventy year mark. This is again why the last week of the seventy years is not fulfilled historically, as the king (Jesus) was crucified instead of crowned; what the angel Gabriel told Daniel would happen to Christ in 69 weeks of years biblically occurred to the Temple in 69 real time years from the birth of Christ.

King David was a prophet as well, in approximately 1000 BC he wrote, *"Dogs have surrounded me, a band of wicked men have encircled me. They pierced my hands and my feet. I can count all my bones. People stare and gloat over me. They divide my garments among them, and cast lots upon my clothing."* - Psalm 22:16-18. He knew that Christ would come from his seed, as he was the first true king over Israel, and the connections to King David and the Messiah are more than DNA, they are symbolic in the lifespan of a king being seventy years. The discourse in Daniel given by the angel Gabriel of sixty-nine weeks for the Messiah to be cut off was exactly fulfilled by not only biblical historical data but on our calendar as well; our current calendar was changed in 525 AD by a Christian monk named Dionysus Exiguus from the previously used Diocletian calendar. He renamed the years prior to the birth of Christ to BC (before Christ) and the years after his birth to AD (Anno Domini, the year of our Lord). After the fulfillment of the 69 real-time years of the destruction of the temple in Jerusalem, it is without a doubt that he was divinely inspired in the accuracy of the birth of Christ. Biblically, there is not any question of when Christ was born, as it had to have been in 1 AD, as seen in the destruction of the temple sixty-nine years after his birth. The continuous controversy over such subjects as the date of his birth and death can be answered through the scriptures in symbolism as the historical data surrounding the aspects of why they would change his birthdate are based on inconclusive evidence such as the death of King Herod; and only further the plan of the secular world in eradicating

Christ, as seen in the only recent changes made on our calendar system using BCE (BC) and CE (AD). When some began to question such subtle aspects of Christianity such as the birth year of the Messiah, by which our current calendar was changed and is kept, it leads to others who claim that the bible could not possibly have been kept intact in exactness. This is Satan's subtle lie; "God did not really say you would die if you ate from that tree?" or "The bible could not really have been preserved all these years without changes being made". We worship the highest most Almighty God; it would be insulting to God to insinuate that he could not preserve and protect his word, as if he were impotent in the schemes of Satan.

The other camp has stated that either all or half of the last week was fulfilled historically. Some feel that all the prophecy was fulfilled historically by the destruction of the temple and later Jerusalem, and the other segment feels that half of the last week was fulfilled in the actual crucifixion of Jesus, and applying the term "abomination that causes desolation" to his death. Regardless of which idea one contemplates, neither is accurate, as the opening statement by Gabriel explains the culmination that occurs after the seventy weeks are fulfilled which will be, *"to put an end to sin, to atone for wickedness, to bring in everlasting righteousness, to seal up vision and prophecy and to anoint the most holy."* None of those prophetic statements have come to pass. Since we have determined that after the sixty-nine weeks, applied to the Messiah being cut off, terminates the end of the weeks of years prophecy to date, then the last week is yet to come.

Three and a Half

There are several different ways in which the timeframe of the seventieth week of apocalypse is presented by John in Revelation, as well as Daniel that explains the division of the last week.

One-half of the Week =Time, times, and half a time [Revelation 12:14, Daniel 12:7]

One-half of the Week=1260 days, 1290 days [Revelation 11:3, 12:6, Daniel 12:11)]

One-half of the Week=42 months [Revelation 11:2, 13:5]

One week [Daniel 9:27]

Most of the descriptions that describe "one half" of the "week", which is three and one half years, are of the second or last half of the seven year tribulation. The only indication in the bible of the first three and one half years is in Daniel 9:27, and 11: 21, as the angel Gabriel describes how the antichrist comes to power, and subsequently comes to an agreement with Israel as a nation; the agreement is a seven year term, and he only keeps one half of the term before he breaks the agreement. The reader can assume from this information that the antichrist establishes his power during the first three and a half years of the tribulation and all seems well with the agreement made with the Israeli people.

We find the latter half of the tribulation in a dizzying scene of apocalyptic proportions, divided between the actions of the antichrist and the false prophet versus the power of God unleashed on the world and specifically the kingdom of the beast.

The phrase of "time, times and half a time" is not only representative of time itself as in three and a half years, but symbolic of the sign that Jesus gave in Matthew 12:39-40, which is the sign of Jonah. Christ was in the earth for three days and three nights, and after his resurrection, he appeared for forty days and then was caught up to heaven. The time, and times is equal to time (one), and times (two) which is equivalent to three days and nights, followed by the forty days being symbolic of the 'half a time'. The same occurred in Jonah after he was vomited on the shore by the fish, in that when God spoke to him again to go to Nineveh, it took him three days to go through the city proclaiming "Forty more days and Nineveh will be destroyed". The 'half a time' is symbolic of the preaching of the Gospel to the unsaved, with time given for repentance. The city of Nineveh repented at his preaching but was ultimately and utterly destroyed at a later date as was told through the prophet Nahum. The vine that grew over Jonah's head was indicative of the symbolism that Jonah was a "Christ type figure"; it sprang up overnight and was destroyed overnight. Jesus gives us the answer to the symbolism twice during his ministry, the first was that he stated that *"no sign shall be given except for the sign of Jonah"* and second, he states, *"I am the vine"* in John 15:5.

The timeframe of 1260 days in Revelation and 1290 days in Daniel are the same sequence of time; the latter has an added month of thirty days, and we know from Revelation that 1260 days is the timespan of Israel fleeing into the desert to a place prepared for her by God. The added month could be their return to Judea; however, it is clear from scriptures that Israel spends the second half of the tribulation in the desert in a place prepared beforehand by God. It is also the amount of time spent prophesying by the 'two witnesses' as depicted in Revelation, in that they are sent by God to preach for 1260 days, or the latter half of the tribulation week. It is during this time, that they unleash the plagues of Egypt on earth by turning water to blood as Moses did, and shutting up the sky so that it will not rain as occurred with Elijah, and to "strike the earth with every kind of plague as often as they want". They preach for exactly 1260 days or *three and a half years*, and then the beast from the Abyss kills them, leaving their bodies lying in the street for *three and a half days*. These passages again have a repetitive cycle of the sign of Jonah, which is three and a half.

The next span of time is given as forty-two months in Revelation. It is a reference to the length of time that the beast or the Antichrist is allowed to exercise his authority, which is the latter half of the seven year tribulation; the reader can assume that this timeframe begins with the breaking of the agreement with the nation of Israel and continues until he is conquered at the return of Christ. He is shown in Daniel as seeking military conquest and pitching his tent between the seas at the beautiful holy mountain; this area geographically is in northern Israel where the plain of Megiddo is located between the Sea of Galilee and the Mediterranean Sea which is at the base of the Mt. Carmel mountain range. Mt. Carmel has historic biblical significance; it is where Elijah competed with the priests of Baal in which they were defeated and put to death.

The last reference to the seven year tribulation occurs in Daniel during the angelic discourse, in which Gabriel states that the Antichrist will confirm a covenant with many for "one seven" meaning seven years, and in the middle of that time (three and a half years) he will put an end to sacrifice and offering. The covenant that he confirms is the Abrahamic covenant, in which the land legally belongs to the Israelis, and the most contested piece of that land is the Temple Mount. In breaking of the "covenant" he stops the sacrificial offerings, which allows the reader to know that the agreement is in reference to the Temple Mount, the Temple, and the right of the Jews to continue their worship there. The breaking of this treaty is acknowledged in Isaiah:

Look, their brave men cry aloud the streets; the envoys of peace weep bitterly. The highways are deserted no travelers are on the roads. The treaty is broken, its witnesses are despised, no one is respected. (Isaiah 33:7-8)

Christians are to be a final witness to the world in the end times of the events unfolding; a preterist or partial preterist viewpoint of the seventieth week of Daniel robs the gospel of its validity when the time arrives for the Antichrist to confirm a covenant with the Jewish people. The world, along with many Christians, will believe that this significant event is nothing more than a benevolent benefactor to the Jewish nation in their time of need, and will overlook the greatest of opportunities to sound a warning before the Antichrist comes to complete power; nor will they be interested in hearing the truth of the prophecies from those who are wise. Once the Antichrist has total authority, the freedom of expressing religious thoughts on his identity will be lost. Preterism is, to coin a phrase, "Biblical Atheism", in which views of future prophetic events are either considered archaic or relegated to superstition, and it ultimately robs the gospel of its infinite truths regarding the Jewish nation, and core Christian beliefs in the return of the Messiah. It is a false doctrine, and the ones who propagate it are false teachers who are content to live without absolute truths; without the absolute truths of the bible, we have relativism; which is defined as 'the truth is only relative to the circumstances'. If the bible isn't absolutely truthfully correct, then Islam, Buddhism, Hinduism, or a myriad of other pagan religions are not wrong; and Christians are no longer the light in a dark world.

Daniel's seventieth week is a prophecy of the future, and that is the how Christians should interpret it, if we are to continue as the light in the world.

Rumors of War

You will hear of wars and rumors of wars,

but see to it that you are not alarmed. Such

things must happen but the end is still to come.

— Matthew 24:6

✦

Chapter 9

A Bloody Century

The end will come like a flood: War will continue until the end and desolations have been decreed. (Daniel 9:26)

A tsunami swept across the globe during the twentieth century, not one of water, but of war. Civil unrest had begun in many countries prior to the year 1900, which led to World War I; the first official worldwide war was declared on July 28, 1914 and lasted until November 11, 1918. The end of the war was officially declared by the signing of the first peace treaty, the Treaty of Versailles, on June 28, 1919 claiming peace between the allied forces and Germany. The treaty was to be followed by many more peaceful negotiations between most countries of the world. Regardless of the paper that it was signed on, it was not able to prevent the bloodiest century of combat that followed in the known history of warfare. The wars that proceeded the peace treaty signing became increasingly violent with deadlier weapons being used in each new conflict.

The crimes which we seek to condemn and punish have been so calculated, so malignant, and so devastating, that a civilization cannot tolerate their being ignored, because it cannot survive their being repeated. – US chief prosecutor Robert Jackson, Opening Address for the United States November 21, 1945 International Military Tribunal, Nuremberg

There were around thirty major global conflicts throughout the duration of the last century including two world wars, with an estimate of approximately 110,000,000 soldier and civilian casualties. With the beginning of the new millennium, the fighting has moved in the direction of the Middle East and the continent of Africa, both of which have a large percentage of Muslim populations. This is in accordance to the body of the leopard or the nation of Islam; it will be the largest segment of the beasts' followers and also the most dangerous. Our media no longer communicates the news accurately or with the freedom of speech allowed in our constitution. They suppress or minimize stories that pertain to Islam, Muslims, and radical Islamic related violence in the US. It only takes one story or movie that depicts radical Islamists in an unfavorable, yet truthful light; and Islamic followers across the globe become inflamed in acts of violent protest. Maybe it is out of fear, or maybe it is the current stance of blind political correctness, no matter what the issue is, that not only the media but our government as well has chosen a path that appears weak in the eyes of predator countries that harbor terrorists. Which citizens have been the most inconvenienced by the politically correct agenda of non-racial profiling in airports? Airport security will go to great lengths to show the public how they will pull an elderly citizen out of their wheelchair at checkpoints; however, a Middle Eastern man can walk through a checkpoint without having to do more than show security their boarding pass. Since Barack Obama came to office, this climate of radically altered American views toward Muslims has increased dramatically. The First Lady, Michelle Obama, was actually quoted as stating, "The only time I have been proud of this country is when my husband was elected as President". This is the wonderful couple that America not only elected once, but twice, to serve our nation as its leader.

The "War on Terror" should be renamed, "The War for America to protect its oil interests in the Middle East". One does not need to be a Wall Street Analyst to figure out, that outside of protecting our strongest Middle Eastern ally, Israel, the only commodity of value for America on that part of the globe is oil.

I looked, and there before me was a black horse. Its rider was holding a pair of scales in his hand. Then I heard what sounded like a voice among the four living creatures saying, "A quart of wheat for a day's wages, and three quarts of barley for a day's wages, and do not damage the oil and the wine!" (Revelation 6:5-6)

Most biblical scholars agree that this verse is in reference to famine, followed by the wealthy not being damaged. However, it is very specific, the oil, meaning the Middle Eastern countries that produce and sell the world's oil supply, and wine meaning the wealthiest wine producing countries. The countries that produce wine, such as the US, France, etc., and oil in places such as Kuwait and Saudi Arabia, are already the wealthiest countries on the globe. It is completely in alignment with prophecy, in that the Islamic nations are followers of the beast, therefore they are spared until the end, and the wealthiest countries that produce wine are spared as well, most likely due to their wealth, and their alliance or affiliation with the beast political system. Since oil was not discovered in the Middle East until the 1908, we have a 'prophecy' in the truest sense of the word, as the book of Revelation was written for the generation upon which these things occur. Although olive oil, which was the original interpretation, was a higher priced commodity in the biblical world, it is now available on every grocery store shelf. Another reason that this is not indicative of olive oil is that oil is used in depicting 'anointing' in scriptures instead of wealth, and we know from Revelation that not all of the anointed are spared in the end times. Should this prophecy refer to olive oil as wealth (of individuals) it would have been more descriptive and logical to use 'perfume' as when the woman poured perfume on Jesus; the passage describes how Judas was appalled and offended because it was so very costly. The scripture, instead, uses a description of a raw or natural commodity or resource that a country produces to obtain its wealth.

It is for this reason that the Middle East has no fear of a "Hiroshima" in their countries; neither the US nor any other country in NATO would deploy weapons of mass destruction against countries where a commodity that is so coveted is located. Sadam Hussein butchered his own people and used chemical weapons against them in remote villages, yet the US did not get involved until he invaded Kuwait and set the oil fields ablaze. The US is protecting her valued resource in the Middle East and the 'War on Terror' is the smokescreen. The US government knows this, and so do the Saudis and Kuwait, and this is the reason why the American government has turned a blind eye towards the atrocities that are committed in the name of their religion, and with the knowledge that Saudi Arabia has supported terrorist organizations, yet we continue to align ourselves with them. Even moderate American Muslim groups openly support Hamas and Hezbollah, though the two groups have direct ties to terroristic activities.

The Truth About Islam

Islam has been presented as a 'Religion of Peace' to the American public, yet the American public has had a difficult time of differentiating between what is presented and what has been done in the name of that religion; the old adage of "actions speak louder than words". The birth of Islam began in violence; the Muslims of Saudi Arabia conquered and converted by the sword. The truth, in the deepest beating heart of Islam, is for the entire world to be under and subject to their god, Allah, by any means necessary. All Muslims want this, just as all Christians would like to see the world converted to Christianity, yet the difference between the two in methods of conversion are in stark contrast. Islam converts by methods of violence and intimidation, the convert has no choice, save one; and once converted, may never again choose another religion. 'Choice' is removed in Islam, as is many human rights elements, especially for women.

The ancient world in which Judaism was born was one of violence, the worship of the ancient deities in Babylon, Sumeria, and other lost cities of the ancient world demanded not only sacrifice, but human sacrifice. The gods, Molech and Marduk, demanded child sacrifice, other deities demanded prostitution in return for fertility, plentiful crop harvests, and other issues of importance to the ancient world. When Abraham was called by God to come out of the land of the Chaldeans, he was called out of the violent demands of the religious deities of that country. It is no coincidence that God asked Abraham to sacrifice his son Isaac, as it was that type of sacrifice that was occurring in Ur. Abraham knew that the God that had begun speaking to him was different than the other gods that were being worshiped, yet when asked to sacrifice his child that was given to him by God; he had the knife raised in mid-air before being stopped by the angel. He didn't hesitate; the other 'gods' demanded this, and God tested Abraham to see if Abraham loved him enough to give God as much as the gods, Molech or Marduk, demanded.

Do not give any of your children to be sacrificed in the fire to Molech; for you must not profane the name of your God, I am the Lord. (Leviticus 18:21)

Child sacrifice was not a 'novel' thing in ancient Chaldea when God asked Abraham to do this; it was a regular occurrence in a religious ritual, though God never would have required Abraham to go through with it. It was still a regular part of religious ritual that had gained footing in Judea under Jeremiah the prophet.

They have built the high place of Topheth in the Valley of Ben Hinnom to burn their sons and daughters in the fire-something I did not command, nor did it enter my mind. (Jeremiah 7:31)

There was a stunning moment of revelation to Abraham upon which Judaism and Christianity is based, a moment in which God stopped him, in which God showed himself different from the other 'gods' that were worshiped, in which God showed mercy and compassion. It is still that stunning moment of revelation that is in undeniable contrast to Islam, that moment of revelation in which Jesus said, *"Go and learn what this means, I desire mercy, not sacrifice".* (Matthew 9:13), and again, *"I desire mercy not sacrifice".* (Hosea 6:6)

It is this mercy that is a great void in Islam. It is that revelation of which, a thousand burnt offerings cannot compare to one act of mercy, in which an eye for an eye is legally just, but the act of mercy is greater. The greatest revelation of the only true God is his ability to show mercy in which the sacrifice he gave, in Christ, provided a way out for the sinner. Under the law, blood must be shed to atone for sin, it is this same concept that prevails in Islam, and their god, Allah, provided no way out for them. Their god, through the Quran, desires blood to atone for sin; it is these Quranic verses that prompt radical Islamist.

Quran (2:191-193) - "And slay them wherever ye find them, and drive them out of the places whence they drove you out, for persecution [of Muslims] is worse than slaughter [of non-believers]... but if they desist, then lo! Allah is forgiving and merciful. And fight them until persecution is no more, and religion is for Allah."

Quran (2:216) - "Fighting is prescribed for you, and ye dislike it. But it is possible that ye dislike a thing which is good for you, and that ye love a thing which is bad for you. But Allah knoweth, and ye know not."

Quran (4:76) - "Those who believe fight in the cause of Allah..."

Quran (4:89) - "They but wish that ye should reject Faith, as they do, and thus be on the same footing (as they): But take not friends from their ranks until they flee in the way of Allah (From what is forbidden). But if they turn renegades, seize them and slay them wherever ye find them; and (in any case) take no friends or helpers from their ranks."

Quran (5:33) - "The punishment of those who wage war against Allah and His messenger and strive to make mischief in the land is only this, that they should be murdered or crucified or their hands and their feet should be cut off on opposite sides or they should be imprisoned; this shall be as a disgrace for them in this world, and in the hereafter they shall have a grievous chastisement"

Quran (8:12) - "I will cast terror into the hearts of those who disbelieve. Therefore strike off their heads and strike off every fingertip of them"

Their god is Molech, under a new identity named Allah. Molech, the god that required a mother and father to sacrifice their child in the fire, in the name of religion still whispers to the worshiper of Allah when it says "Your son should give his life for jihad, your son will be in paradise afterwards." In an online video showing the realities of radical Islam, one mother had given four sons in suicide bombings, she was honored by her people; she stated that should she have ten sons, she would sacrifice them all for Allah. The deeper truth is that mankind desires blood, and learned to use religion as its guise. The first born child on planet earth committed murder. Cain shedding the blood of his brother was indicative of mankind's journey on this planet. The Roman Catholic Church desired power and the shedding of blood made them feel powerful, they had learned to use religion to commit murder and not be held accountable by human standards. Though Islam was a newer religion in the Middle East, as opposed to the ancient religions of Babylon and Sumeria, it is not a new religion; it is an old religion with new laws. The Middle East is famous for the invention of the laws of a society; the Code of Hammurabi was an ancient legal code that was written in about 1772 BC in ancient Babylon, in which 282 laws were enacted by King Hammurabi under his reign that covered all aspects of society from taxes paid, to an eye for an eye form of justice. Laws in and of themselves are not wrong, provided that they show mercy for a transgressor; should we have a society that does not adhere to "Thou shall not kill", anyone could commit murder without even needing justification. Some Christians believe that with the

Crucifixion, the law was abolished, but Christ said, *"I did not come to abolish the law or the prophets, but to fulfill it" (Matthew 5:17)*, though some Christians believe the law was abolished, they still abide by the Ten Commandments. Was the Law abolished after Christ came? The answer is no, the second part of his statement was that he came to fulfill it. The fulfilling was the sacrificial aspect of Judaism, in that to atone for man's sin, a blood sacrifice must be made. The verses in the Old Testament Law that pertain to Judaism, in which God was exemplifying the Jews as a separate and Holy People unto him as a model to the pagan nations around them was symbolic of Holiness versus Paganism, such laws as dietary restrictions on clean and unclean foods were the equivalent of the saying "you are what you eat". God wanted to contrast the Jews which were called to be separate and holy, from the pagan peoples who subscribed to "detestable" practices, in that the pagan people were "separated" from God. The abolishment of this practice by the Judeo Christian converts was the abolishment of the symbolism related to it, in which Gentiles were 'unclean' and Jews were 'clean'.

He saw heaven opened and something like a large sheet being let down to earth by its four corners. It contained all kinds of four footed animals as well as reptiles of the earth and birds of the air. Then a voice told him, "Get up Peter, kill and eat." "Surely not, Lord!" Peter replied. "I have never eaten anything impure or unclean". The voice spoke to him a second time, "Do not call anything impure that God has made clean." (Acts 10:11)

You are well aware that it is against our law for a Jew to associate with a Gentile or visit him. But God has shown me that I should not call any man impure or unclean. (Acts 10:28)

Under Christ there is no clean and unclean, for the things that made Gentiles unclean were atoned for in the blood of Christ. The second verse also rebukes racism of any kind, as all peoples are created by God. In the crucifixion of Christ, his blood made atonement for all encompassing sin of the believer, and the Old Testament laws and regulations that are no longer adhered to by Christians is the result of them not so much abolished as they no longer exist, the power that sacrifice had in Old Testament times no longer has power, it is like a gun without bullets. In a simplistic symbolic example; a pregnant woman takes extra care of herself during her pregnancy, she takes prenatal vitamins, and hopefully abstains from drugs, alcohol, and other things that would harm the fetus. Most women, after having the baby resume a regular lifestyle; they do not continue to make preparations for a birth that has already occurred. The Jewish nation was pregnant prior to the birth of Christ; they are now the mother who does not believe her child has come; they are the equivalent of a woman having a false pregnancy. After the crucifixion of Christ, until 70AD, they continued to make sacrifices at the temple. These sacrifices were not "right or wrong"; they were simply empty of power, as if they were firing a gun with no bullet. The fact that God examines the motives of men clearly defines that presenting a temple sacrifice to God is not wrong as long as the motive is pure and not purely duty, as God acknowledges that the Jewish nation has been temporarily blinded as to the Messiah in John 12:40.

The laws that pertain to the Old Testament of religious legal codes were rendered impotent by Christ, in that mercy surpasses the law; and the same with the believer, who after giving their life to Christ, sin becomes impotent in their life in their striving to be Christ-like in nature have not the desire to willingly commit sin. When a Christian commits a sin, the mercy shown by Christ in his blood covers the sin, therefore, from a religious legal standpoint, the sin does not get what it wants, which is legally imposed punishment on the believer. The law of the land is different however, and the legal justice system is upheld in the physical world, sometimes with mercy, and sometimes without, as in a judge showing leniency on the lawbreaker.

With Islam, a person not only has a god that does not show mercy on a "sinner" but also the legalism of their religious law is upheld by the adherents of Islam in which they do not show each other mercy. There is no sacrifice to atone for their "sins" except the blood of the sinner themselves. Islam is a man-made religion without mercy, which desires bloodshed through its followers. For those who believe we are all serving the same God with different names, the glaring differences between Christianity and Islam should be obvious.

So why have so many pointed out the similarities between the Old Testament violence and the Quran? In the previous chapter, Animal Planet, the origins of Islam were discussed with regards to the false prophet

Mohammed and his initial introduction to Christianity with a Christian monk; Islam is based on some of the original teachings of the Old Testament and the other part fabrications. Islam acknowledges many aspects of Christianity; the patriarchal father Abraham, the prophets, but only recognizes Jesus as a prophet. The Quran also acknowledges the bible, called only 'the book', and many end time revelations of the Quran correspond almost exactly to the book of Revelation itself. Judaism is the oldest amongst the three religions of Judaism, Christianity, and Islam; the birth of Christianity in 1 AD, with the written historical secular evidence proves that Christians are adherents of a much older predicated religion which was Judaism, yet Islam, not formed until 622 AD, claims that Jesus was a prophet of Islam which is impossible as Islam was formed six hundred years after the birth of Christ. The secular evidence from sources outside of the bible has proof of the dates of Christian origin and traditional Judaism through writings from all of the governments that had ever ruled over Judea including Rome, yet Islam makes the wild claims that they are the only true religion. Islam has warped its religion and belief system into a pretzel; they deny Christianity yet claim Jesus is a prophet of their religion, yet their religion was not formed until six hundred years after the birth of Christ. It becomes even more complicated as they deny Judaism, and the right of Israel to exist in the land of Judea of which they claim ancestral hood from the patriarch Abraham; claiming that Ishmael was the chosen son not Isaac, but if Israel doesn't belong there, then why do they acknowledge Isaac as a son of Abraham; whether or not he was the chosen child, they still admit he existed. They also acknowledge all of the Jewish prophets of the Old Testament from Judaism, which they claim is a 'false religion'. When asking a 'moderate Muslim' if they think violence is a good thing in their religion, they say 'no', so they are not adhering to the holy book of their religion and the commands of the god therein. The contradictions could go on and on…to summarize; Islam is a false man-made religion that Satan is using as his 'seeds' which he has sown into the world.

Who is Gog?

Ezekiel was a prophet to Israel when they were exiled in Babylonian captivity. The beginning of the book deals with Israel's sins and the reason why they were placed in captivity, but during the final chapters of Ezekiel, the book becomes chronological, in chapters thirty-seven onwards, of a future time for Israel based on four separate segments. The first segment begins in chapter 37; it is a vision called the valley of dry bones, and it pertained to a time in Israel's future many millennia later. Ezekiel sees a valley filled with dry bones, which represents 'dead men'; God tells Ezekiel to prophesy to the dry bones, and when Ezekiel did, flesh appeared on them and breath entered them, and they stood on their feet, a vast army. Some view this as the nation of Israel coming back to the land of Judea; however, of all peoples separated from their homelands, the Jewish nation has held to their traditions the tightest; they were still alive as a nation in distant lands. This verse reverberates with symbolism of the nation of Israel being brought to the point of death or extinction. This verse speaks specifically and prophetically about the holocaust; the survivors of the Holocaust were as dead men coming back to life. The second segment begins in the middle of chapter 37 and describes the regathering of Israel back to the land of Judea joining them as one nation undivided. The biblical Israelites were a divided nation, with the northern kingdom of Samaria, and the southern kingdom, which included Judah. Both segments of this prophecy have been fulfilled beginning in 1933 and Hitler's rise to power, through 1967 when the Israelis captured East Jerusalem during the Six Day War. They have been a united nation since the rebirth of their country, in fighting for their right to exist as a sovereign nation. Since chapter thirty-seven is chronological, and the remainder of the chapters in Ezekiel have not been fulfilled historically, the reader can draw the conclusion that the subsequent verses that proceed chapter thirty-seven are also in chronological order.

The third segment begins in chapter thirty-eight with Ezekiel receiving revelation from God regarding an alliance of nations that advance upon Israel, after their restoration as a nation. The prophecy is very specific, and can only be referred to Israel in its current state, as opposed to the end of Christ's millennial reign or as the Battle of Armageddon. A key specific scripture as to the timeframe of this event is as follows:

Get ready; be prepared, you and all the hordes gathered about you, and take command of them. After many days you will be called to arms. In future years you will invade a land that has recovered from war, whose people were gathered from many

nations to the mountains of Israel, which had long been desolate.
They had been brought out from the nations, and now all of them
live in safety. (Ezekiel 38: 7-8)

Israel today matches this particular verse exactly, the war they recovered from was World War II, and then they were gathered back to Israel in 1948. They live in safety to the effect that they will not be invaded and conquered by another nation, as they have NATO support and the US as an ally, plus they control their own country, whereas the previous 500 years that they lived in Jerusalem before being banished was under the control of other empires from Babylon to Rome.

There are several different opinions of who God is referring to when he tells Ezekiel to "set his face against Gog"; some expositors have drawn the conclusion that this verse refers to Russia, however when this prophecy was written in the sixth century BC, Russia was largely uninhabited and had not yet been named, so if prophesying of a future "Russia" then the actual word "Russia" should have been used, but Ezekiel was supposed to "face the north" and prophesy against them during his lifetime. Also, the world was still living in the "cradle of civilization", so the reference to the far north, would only extend to the most inhabited northern nations of the known world, which was Turkey in Ezekiel's time. When casually reading the passage, one might assume that "Gog" refers to a place geographically, however under intense study; the verse does not allude to a place, but a person.

Son of man, set your face against Gog, of the land of Magog, the chief prince of Meshech and Tubal. (Ezekiel 38:2)

Gog is an entity in which God says to set his face against; Gog is the chief prince of Meshech and Tubal in the land of Magog. The term "chief prince" gives Gog an identity, but who is it? First, the reader needs to understand the location, where the land of Magog is located. Noah had three sons, Ham, Shem and Japheth; and Japheth had seven sons, of which four of them were Gomer, Magog, Tubal and Meshech. These were some of the post-divulian people who repopulated the earth after the flood. The locations of where they lived settled and built new cities were named after them. The historical locations of those places are in what is now modern Turkey. Drawing the conclusion that Turkey is *"the land of Magog"*, we can now try to ascertain who Gog is, as we know that he or it is an enemy of God. This can be accomplished by examining other scriptures to determine the "chief prince" of Turkey. Prince, in the bible, can either be a country's leader, as in Daniel 11:22 as a *"prince of the covenant"* referring to a leader of the nation of Israel; or a celestial being such as in Daniel 12:1, in which *"Michael, the great prince who protects your people"* is a celestial being who is in charge of the people of Israel, and Satan described as *"the prince of this world"* in John 12:31. Gog is described as a "chief prince", the reading of the passage seems to describe a celestial rather than human prince as Ezekiel was to prophesy to him in his lifetime, yet the actual fulfillment of the prophecy would not occur for several millennia. Though he is of celestial nature, he is an enemy of

God. There are further verses to describe the "spiritual realm" of Turkey in Revelation, such as when Jesus is addressing the church of Pergamum, which is on the coast of western Turkey.

I know where you live, where Satan has his throne. (Revelation 2:13)

These were the words of Jesus, so the reader knows them to be accurate in the actual location of "Satan's throne" on earth in the spiritual realm. It is also the most likely location for the future antichrist to emerge, and it was the locations of the empires that ruled over Judea in the metal statue in that Babylon and Assyria had extended control of Turkey. Magog, in Hebrew, is defined as "covering or rooftop", as in a covering for an abode or dwelling, and "Gog" in Hebrew means "mountain"; mountain is symbolic of a kingdom. Should the passage be interpreted this way, we have: "*The kingdom of the chief prince that covers the dwelling in which Satan has his throne in the land of Meshech and Tubal (Turkey)*". God is specifically calling it the "kingdom of Satan".

For we wrestle not against flesh and blood, but against principalities, against powers, against the rulers of the darkness of this world, against spiritual wickedness in high places (Ephesians 6:12)

It is no coincidence that the Middle East has been engulfed in conflict, has a false and pagan religious system, and Muslims commit atrocities against their own families such as honor killing. The place in which they reside is the equivalent of moving next door to a nuclear waste facility; before too long, the people develop sicknesses associated with their environment. The environment in the Middle East of the spiritual essence has caused the people there to develop a "spiritual sickness". The reality of this situation is their intense hatred of Jews, Christians, and Americans whom they view as "Christian". The Middle Eastern Muslims are slowly being poisoned by their spiritual environment. The reason Turkey has remained off the "radar" in the Middle East with involvement of radical Islamists, is a calculated move by its spiritual protector; that is the "covering". Turkey is being preserved for a future scenario as the country that not only invades Israel, but also brings forth the final beast; however, it does not stay off the radar as seen in Ezekiel thirty-eight.

I will turn you around put hooks in your jaws and bring you out with your whole army-your horses, your horsemen fully armed, and a great horde with large and small shields, all of them brandishing their swords. (Ezekiel 38:4)

The phrasing of this passage is indicative of what "Gog" is being viewed as; the important word here is "hooks". There are other passages of scripture that should be read to get a clear picture of what God is calling "Gog".

Because you rage against me and your insolence has reached my ears, I will put my hook in your nose and my bit in your mouth and I will make you return by the way you came. (2 Kings 19:28)

This particular scripture is describing the actions God took against Sennacherib, the Assyrian King who came against Jerusalem during the reign of King Hezekiah in Israel. It is phrased exactly opposite of the preceding verse, in that the Assyrian came against Israel and God dragged him away by putting a hook in his nose. Though Sennacherib left Israel, and was subsequently murdered by his sons; the locations of the Assyrian Empire with its peoples still exist in the Middle East. The boundaries of Assyria are the rivers of Tigris and Euphrates to the middle of modern Turkey which included Tubal and probably Meshech as well. God is calling these modern nations by their ancient names; therefore the invaders to come are referred to by their ancient name as well. Paraphrased, this is what God is saying:

"I put my hook in your nose and my bit in your mouth and made you turn around and leave Israel (between 705-681 BC) and in future years I will turn you around again and put my hook in your mouth and bring you against Israel with your entire army."

It is non-specific to a particular "ruler" such as Sennacherib was; instead, it is towards "Gog"; the spiritual force over those specific territories, which is now entwined with Islam. Consider the following passage when deciding whether the past relates to a future event:

Whatever is has already been, and what will be has been before; and God will call the past to account. (Ecclesiastes 3:15)

The confederation that invades Israel includes Tubal, Meshech, Gomer, and Togarmah; all of which are located in Turkey, along with Persia, Put and Cush which are the modern countries of Iraq, Libya, and

Ethiopia, Iran could also be included as a part of ancient Persia as one cannot imagine a multi-coalition invasion of Israel without having Iran involved, however, Madai or "Medes", as in the Median Empire, was not specified in these scriptures. The entire armies of invaders are killed on the mountains of northern Israel by a supernatural event, of which God says *"And I will show my greatness and my holiness, and I will make myself known in the sight of many nations. Then they will know that I am the Lord."* *(Ezekiel 38:23).* This coincides exactly to the events that happened in antiquity with regards to Sennacherib's army, as they were slayed by an angel during the night in their encampment. God destroyed the original Assyrian army by supernatural means, and he will do so again on the mountains of Israel during this invasion.

Some believe this event is the battle of Armageddon; this is an incorrect interpretation of scriptures, as the last days of Israel during Daniel's seventieth week will not be lived in peace and culminates with the Jewish nation fleeing to the mountains for safety. It states in Ezekiel that these nations notice that Israel is living in peace and safety.

On that day thoughts will come into your mind and you will devise an evil scheme. You will say, "I will invade a land of unwalled villages, I will attack a peaceful and unsuspecting people-all of them living without walls and without gates and bars. (Ezekiel 38:10-11)

In that day, when my people Israel are living in safety, will you not take notice of it? You will come from your place in the far north,

you and many nations with you all of them riding on horses a
great horde, a mighty army. You will advance against my people
Israel like a cloud that covers the land. (Ezekiel 38:14-16)

Furthermore, when the army is destroyed the Israelis
will collect the weapons of the fallen army and use
them as a fuel source for seven years. Ezekiel
describes that the Israelis will be regularly employed to
locate human remains and bury them for seven
months in the Valley of Hamon Gog (translated from
Hebrew as Valley of the hordes of Gog). This is not the
actions of a people living in Christ's millennial reign;
and last:

All the people of the land will bury them, and the day I am
glorified will be a memorable day for them, declares the Sovereign
Lord. (Ezekiel 39:13)

After God has performed this miracle by slaying the
invading army, the people of Israel will be regularly
employed to bury the dead, and cleanse the land. They
will scout the land and wherever they find bones, they
will set up a marker for others to come and bury the
body. The nation as a whole will set the date of their
deliverance as a memorial day in Israel and will be
commemorated each year. Also, as in other events
listed in the bible, should there be no reference to the
return of Christ, or the resurrection of the dead, then,
one should not assume that these events are a
portrayal of the last battle or Armageddon. This
invasion is an Islamic coalition that invades Israel in
the future, but is not incorporated into Daniel's
seventieth week, as it occurs before.

The fourth segment occurs after the description of this invasion of Israel; beginning in chapter forty are visions of the third and final temple to be built in Jerusalem. As was discussed in the previous chapter, the third temple will be built before the return of Christ and is either built after this invasion occurs, or the invasion is a result of the temple being built. The two events could also be many years apart. The angel goes into great detail regarding the dimensions of the temple and how temple service and worship is to be conducted. For those who are of the opinion that the temple will be rebuilt after the return of Christ, there would be no reason for any of the specifics to be included in this description; but Ezekiel is giving the nation of Israel a blueprint or drafting design for the temple. He also goes into great detail regarding the priestly duties, and the clothing of the priests.

What the locust swarm has left the great locusts have eaten; what the great locusts have left the young locusts have eaten what the young locusts have left the other locusts have eaten. (Joel 4:1)

Joel is a book of prophetic writings based on the future of Israel from the viewpoint of the author, which was Joel, writing in the ninth or eighth century BC. The entire book of Joel encompasses the future, as Joel was a prophet to Israel prior to the first invasion of Israel by Babylon. Some expositors feel that this verse is describing a locust plague that devastated Israel historically, however, the locusts described here are symbolic of the future invasions of Israel by Gentile nations that attacked Israel in such numbers as to appear as a swarm of locusts that devour everything in their path.

The first locust swarm was Babylon, and they not only destroyed Jerusalem and the temple, but also carried the Israelites into exile; the great locusts were the Assyrians under Sennacherib, although he did not sack Jerusalem, he deported much of the northern kingdom of Israel to others lands and overran their outlying towns of Judea. The young locusts were the Greeks, who first conquered and made Israel subject to the Grecian Empire under Alexander the Great, and were followed by several centuries of Seleucid rule. The other locusts in this verse were the Romans, the last empire to dominate Israel before the Jews were banished from their own country.

This was spoken to Joel by the Lord, at least two centuries before the first invasion occurred, however Joel was not describing the future insomuch as the past from a present day Israel standpoint. Joel described the history of Israel in that short verse, and then moves forward into the time of Israel when the last days occur. He is sounding a warning to Israel of a future invasion when they are re-established as a nation:

Wake up you drunkards, and weep! Wail all you drinkers of wine; wail because of the new wine, for it has been snatched from your lips. A nation has invaded my land, powerful and without number. (Joel 1:5-6)

The new wine is symbolic for the new nation of Israel living in prosperity in their homeland again; much like Jesus stating that you do not put old wine in new wineskins; and the invasion occurs in the middle of drought and famine that will be occurring worldwide during the last days. Joel speaks of the "day of the Lord" being near in Joel 1:15, and then continues the monologue of the actions of the invading armies; from Joel's view, he is describing a modern invasion; modern military warfare has the ability to cause this destruction by their weapons of mass destruction.

Like dawn spreading across the mountains, a large and mighty army comes, such as never was of old nor ever will be in ages to come. Before them fire devours, behind them a flame blazes. Before them the land is like the Garden of Eden, behind them a desert waste-nothing escapes them. (Joel 2:2-3)

Historical combat was not an organized event until the Romans invented the concept of legions; and modern military assemblies are much the same, with the exception of new technology. The invasion that Joel *describes is an organized modern military outfit:*

They charge like warriors; they scale walls like soldiers, they all march In lIne, nol swerving from their course each marches straight ahead. They plunge through defenses without breaking ranks, they rush upon the city; they run along the wall; they climb into the houses; like thieves they enter through the windows. (Joel 2:7-9)

When this invasion occurs, the world is already more than half way through Daniel's seventieth week. These verses correspond to Zechariah's last chapter:

A day of the Lord is coming when your plunder will be divided among you. I will gather all the nations to Jerusalem to fight against it; the city will be captured the houses ransacked, and the women raped. Half of the city will go into exile, but the rest of the people will not be taken from the city. The Lord will go out and fight against those nations, as he fights in the day of battle. (Zechariah 14:1-3)

Whenever the scriptures speak of 'gather all nations to Jerusalem to fight against it', it is in reference to the last battle or Armageddon. The people who choose to remain in Jerusalem instead of fleeing to the mountains will endure the pillage of the city, and some will be deported to other countries. This coincides with the scriptures in Isaiah and Luke of future Jewish exiles into other nations;

In that day the lord will reach out his hand a second time to reclaim the remnant that is left of his people from Assyria, from Lower and Upper Egypt, from Cush from Elam, from Babylonia, from Hamath and from the islands of the sea. (Isaiah 11:11)

They will fall by the sword and will be taken as prisoners to all the nations. (Luke 21:24)

This will be the plight of Israel in the last days, in the latter half of the seven year tribulation; it will not be in peace and safety, but terror and bloodshed for those who do not choose to be refugees in the desert. Three and a half years may not appear to be an extensive amount of time, unless the conditions a person is forced to live in during that time are intolerable; causing three and a half years to seem like decades. The Jewish nation will once again be torn apart for three and a half years, until Christ returns for the final harvest of the earth.

The Omega

"I am the Alpha and the Omega" says the Lord God

"Who is and who was, and who is to come, the

Almighty."

- Revelation 1:8

Chapter 10

✠

Preterism vs. Pre-Millennialism

Immediately after the distress of those days, the sun will be darkened and the moon will not give its light; the stars will fall from the sky and the heavenly bodies will be shaken. (Matthew 24:29)

Throughout the New Testament, the reader is told to watch for the return of Christ, because we do not know on what day he will return. This has led to the notion of the pre-tribulation rapture, in which pre-trib believers think the Lord will return at any given moment. The term "watch" means to be aware of; the lack of discerning the Holy Scriptures in the proper context is the driving force behind many problems with Christianity today. The first problem is the pre-tribulation rapture theory, that has no scriptural verses to confirm it, yet it has been preached as sound doctrine for over a century and has become so grounded in modern theology that to dispute it equals heresy for those who believe it. It has led to the "date setters", which have troubled Christianity for more than a century, but more so in the latter years in North American congregations; the result of date setting is the ridicule of the church by the world. The second problem that faces modern Christianity is preterism, or the general belief that the bible had finished speaking by the end of the first century AD, and that all biblical references are of historical value only. For the modern preterist, there is no room for prophecy, or faith as they believe that Christ returned in 70AD spiritually only and that his kingdom has been progressing for the past two millennia without his physical earthly reign.

Both of these groups are in for serious disappointments. Disillusionment can be unbearable at times, especially spiritual disillusionment, however, for those who believe in the pre-trib rapture, they are only to blame themselves as we are commanded to "test everything"; if a doctrine does not hold up under scriptural examination, then to believe it would be foolhardy. For those hoping to be "removed" from the circumstances of the tribulation, disillusionment will be the price they pay. For those reading this, who believe in the pre-trib rapture, please research it further in scriptures, as you will find there are no supporting biblical verses for a pre-trib rapture, but there are many post-trib verses including the words of Jesus in Matthew 24:29-31, and to test everything as commanded in 1 Thessalonians 5.

Those who hold to the teaching of a post-tribulation rapture are not apocalyptic 'nuts' that want to see devastation to the earth or to other people, they have only discerned from scriptures that it is the reality as portrayed by Jesus himself, and do not want to see their brothers and sisters in Christ become disillusioned. Testing everything applies to the teachings and doctrines of educated clergymen as well.

For those who adhere to preterism, the tribulation will be a shock more than a disappointment. When someone does not believe in something, and it occurs anyway; it will usually be followed by some form of denial. Denial of a situation does not make it disappear, which could lead a person into making poor decisions with lack of understanding. Preterism in itself is a form of denial, it is for those who for whatever moral or personal reasons chose Christianity, are yet denying the gospel in its truest form. They have chosen this path to escape disappointment, this information is actually listed on their website; *International Preterist Association (IPA)*, and is portrayed as the reason preterism exists in that the unfulfilled portions of prophecy that Christians are commanded to expectantly watch and wait for, are too disappointing in their yet unfulfillment.

What is the Preterist View of Bible Prophecy?

Prediction after prediction has failed to materialize, and false hope after false hope has been foisted upon the Christian community. Many Christians have been disillusioned, and are already looking for more reasonable explanations. Some have been so disillusioned they left the faith altogether. It (Preterism) is beginning to capture significant public attention, and is "spreading like wildfire" at the grass roots level. Christ's kingdom is here now. Paradise has been restored in Christ (spiritually-speaking). Christ has conquered all His enemies and has given us the Kingdom.
- David Curtis (IPA)

There are a few scriptures which readily come to mind:

But we are not of those who shrink back and are destroyed. (Hebrews 10:39)

But the cowardly, the unbelieving, the vile, the murderers, the sexually immoral, those who practice magic arts, the idolaters and all liars--they will be consigned to the fiery lake of burning sulfur. This is the second death. (Revelation 21:8)

Holding to a form of godliness, yet denying its power. (2 Timothy 3:5)

The last enemy to be destroyed is death. (1 Corinthians 15:26)

Do your best to present yourself to God as one approved, a worker who does not need to be ashamed and who correctly handles the word of truth. Avoid godless chatter, because those who indulge in it will become more and more ungodly. Their teaching will spread like gangrene. Among them are Hymenaeus and Philetus, who have departed from the truth. They say that the resurrection has already taken place, and they destroy the faith of some. (2 Timothy 2:15-18)

Is Preterism a cowardly view? Are those who adhere to a form of Christianity, but deny its power of prophecy shrinking back from the command given by Jesus himself when he said; "*So you also must be ready, because the Son of Man will come at an hour when you do not expect him.*"(Matthew 24:44). What are we to be ready for? Preterism states that the "resurrection of the dead" has already occurred in 70 AD spiritually; when one distorts scripture in this way, he or she is no longer "with us", "*if whoever is not against you is for you, then whoever is against you is not for you*", see (*Luke 9:49-50*) The cowardly and unbelieving will be thrown into the lake of fire, this is a serious concept, and should a preterist read this…much thought should be given to those views, as it is the eternal soul that is in jeopardy. The gospel, when viewed as only a historical record or allegorically poetic, becomes nothing more than a book of historical facts and dates; and has no power as the living Word of God in an individual's life. A theological professor was asked what his views on preterism were; he stated, "Preterism is like the kitty litter box, someone eventually has to clean it out but no one wants to deal with it".

Lord of the Harvest

There is a time for everything and a season for every activity under heaven, a time to plant and a time to harvest, a time for war and a time for peace. (Ecclesiastes 3:1-2, 8)

Planting is done in the spring, during the summer season the crop grows, and then it is harvested in the autumn. The planting of seeds occurred during the ministry of Jesus and was furthered by his apostles and the written New Testament; Christianity grew during the two millennia since his resurrection, and the harvest occurs in autumn, the end of the age, at the return of Christ. Sewing and reaping is the symbolism used by Jesus to explain the kingdom of God through parables; however there are different types of harvests, especially at the end of the age. Wheat is always used to symbolize a Christian; it is the product of living a Christian life; this is illustrated through the parable of the 'Wheat and the Tares':

The kingdom of heaven is like a man who sowed good seed in his field. But while everyone was sleeping, his enemy came and sowed weeds among the wheat, and went away. When the wheat sprouted and formed heads, the weeds appeared also. (Matthew 13:24-26)

The one who sowed the good seed is the son of Man. The field is the world, and the good seed stands for the sons of the kingdom. The weeds are the sons of the evil one, and the enemy who sows them is the devil. The harvest is the end of the age, and the harvesters are angels. (Matthew 13:37)

There are two separate harvests that occur at the end of the age; the first harvest which is the harvest of 'first fruits', is of the wheat. In Israel, wheat is planted in autumn and grows throughout winter and spring; it is harvested in summer around May. It is during this harvest that the wheat is separated from the tares, and the tares are tied in bundles to be burned. The separation of wheat from tares is more than symbolic, it literally occurs in which the righteous are removed in what is called the rapture or catching up. The angelic harvesters are commanded to sound the trumpet and collect the saints from the four corners of the earth. This is at the end of the age, not of a pre-tribulation rapture; however the harvest of wheat is separate from the second harvest.

The signs of the imminent return of Christ are given by him in his apocalyptic discourse in Matthew 24:29, which will be preceded by many events occurring in

Jerusalem and other places. The sun, moon and stars not giving their light are an immediate precursor to his return; this is an undeniable celestial event that will leave no doubt that something is wrong in the heavens. The true rapture will not be an event done in secret in which millions disappear from earth leaving others wondering what had happened, it will not only be witnessed by those remaining, but everyone will know exactly why it is occurring.

At that time the sign of the Son of Man will appear in the sky, and all the nations of the earth will mourn. They will see the Son of Man coming on the clouds of the sky, with power and great glory. And he will send his angels with a loud trumpet call, and they will gather his elect from the four winds, from one end of the heavens to the other. (Matthew 24:30-31)

He will be recognized by everyone, all the nations of the earth will mourn. He sends his angels, which are the harvesters, to collect his elect; it is during this time that the true church is separated from the imposters. In Zechariah, we find further description of the day the Lord returns as connected to Matthew for the celestial signs.

On that day there will be no light, no cold or frost. It will be a unique day, without daytime or nighttime, a day known to the Lord. When evening comes, there will be light. (Zechariah 14:6-7)

The rapture or catching up of the saints is one of two harvests of the earth.

The Valley of Decision

Armageddon has been the most renowned battle since its penned conception in 95 AD. It has been written about, talked about, fictionalized, taken out of context, but its meaning has been beyond the grasp of more than a few. Some use the word Armageddon to describe the end of the world, while others may think it is the last war, or World War III; it is neither; the word Armageddon is derived from a location in Israel, the valley of Megiddo, where many battles have taken place in the past. The truth is; Armageddon is a harvest that occurs in the autumn of mankind, it is the second harvest of the earth.

I looked, and there before me was a white cloud, and seated on the cloud was one like a son of man, with a crown of gold on his head and a sharp sickle in his hand. Then another angel came out of the temple and called in a loud voice to him who was sitting on the cloud, "Take your sickle and reap, because the time to reap has come, for the harvest of the earth is ripe." (Revelation 14:14)

Swing the sickle, for the harvest is ripe. Come trample the grapes for the winepress is full and the vats overflow so great is the wickedness! Multitudes, multitudes in the valley of decision! For the day of the Lord is near in the valley of decision. (Joel 3:13-14)

This is the second harvest, it is the harvest of grapes which is equated with wickedness, grapes produce wine, and God said of the third horseman to 'not touch the oil or the wine'. It is symbolic of the wealth of royalty, the riches of kings and princes, and those who gather themselves against the returning Christ. The grape harvest in Israel occurs in July through September, which would be after the harvest of the wheat. Throughout this chapter, exact months and times of harvests are only used as a symbolic gesture and in no way does this book encourage the reader to affirm the season or month of the return of Christ. It is simply used as the symbolism that the rapture will occur before the Battle of Armageddon. The scriptures in Revelation 14:14-20 concur with Joel in that the Battle of Armageddon is the harvest of the grapes. Joel calls the valley of Megiddo, the valley of decision; aptly named as the armies gathered there have decided to follow the beast, therefore there is not any that will be spared in that valley, as they are all against Jesus as the returning king.

They are trampled in the winepress outside the city and blood flowed out of the press rising as high as the horses' bridles. (Revelation 14:20)

What eventually befalls this unholy army is something out of a zombie apocalypse movie. When first reading this passage, the average Christian can understand how modern warfare plays a part in this horror scene. In ages past, weapons of warfare were not advanced enough to create the damage described in Zechariah. The ancient prophet describes a plague that is used on the armies of the Antichrist that fight against Jerusalem; he states, *"their flesh will rot while they are still standing on their feet, their eyes will rot in their*

sockets, and their tongues will rot in their mouths"
(Zechariah 14:12).

A similar weapon like this already exists in the
capacity of modern warfare:

*White phosphorus—also known as Willy Pete or Whiskey Pete—is
used by the military for signaling, screening, and incendiary
purposes. White phosphorus munitions, upon explosion, distribute
particles over a wide swath of area. They burn spontaneously in
the air and will continue to burn until all white phosphorus
particles have disappeared. The smoke easily penetrates clothing
and protective gear and can burn a person's flesh to the bone.*

*According to Jeff Englehart, a US soldier involved in the siege of
Fallujah, "Phosphorus burns bodies, in fact it melts the flesh all the
way down to the bone.... Phosphorus explodes and forms a cloud.
Anyone within a radius of 150 meters is done for."*

*Pentagon Confirms Use of White Phosphorus against 'Enemy
Combatants' - The Pentagon, however, does not deny that the
weapon was used against human targets. On November 14, 2005,
spokesman Lieutenant Colonel Barry Venables says that white
phosphorus was used to "fire at the enemy." He adds: "It burns....
It's an incendiary weapon. That is what it does." "It was used as
an incendiary weapon against enemy combatants."*

Rot means to putrefy the flesh, and though "burning"
is not stated in scripture, the burning of flesh without
flames present would appear as "rotting on their feet".
White phosphorus does not affect clothing, only the
skin underneath; graphic pictures of victims of white
phosphorus show the different degrees of burns on the
flesh. The mildest appeared as bullet or bb holes in the

flesh of a survivor; the casualties have skin melted off or charred to ash, and in some, the bones as well; leaving legs and arms as bony stumps instead of hands and feet. When inhaled; white phosphorus burns the tongue, throat, and lungs leaving a victim to be "torched" from the inside out. It works like an airborne acid, except the only thing it burns is human flesh.

According to Zechariah, the soldiers are stricken by confusion from a supernatural source which results in them attacking each other; one possibility is that this sort of confusion would lead to the gathered armies accidentally using these chemical weapons upon each other; or it could be an entirely supernatural event.

The harvest of the grapes is violent; it is the harvest of the enemies of God. The first action of Jesus as returning King is to subdue or destroy his enemies. In 1 Corinthians 15:25-28, Paul states that when Christ returns, he will reign until he has put all his enemies under his feet. "*The last enemy to be destroyed is death.*" Have the Preterists stopped dying? By their own admissions, they have condemned their theology according to Paul. Christ will reign for 1,000 years, and during this time, he will bring everything on the planet under submission. The free will of man will continue to exist; therefore the stipulations are put forth in the Old Testament as to what is expected for all nations under his reign; however, the people living under the reign of Christ have one advantage over those before them, in that the deceiver, Satan, will be bound in chains during the entire time.

When the 1,000 years are finished, Satan will be released from his prison and will go out to deceive the nations once again to gather them for battle against Jesus, but fire comes down from heaven and they are destroyed. Then Satan is thrown into the lake of burning sulphur where he, along with the Beast and the False Prophet, will be tormented for all eternity. Everyone has an eternity, the difference is for those who have accepted Christ, it will be spent in the Kingdom of our Lord; and for those who did not; it will be spent in the company of Satan, the Beast and the False Prophet; tormented forever. Some areas of scriptures are metaphors; the burning lake of fire is not one of them; it is the second death, the death of the immortal soul, and it is for anyone whose name is not found in the Book of Life. The eternal soul will never die, the choices made now, in a human body will affect your eternity; the second death continues forever in torment. Last, death and Hades are thrown into the lake of fire; it is the final enemy of God to be destroyed.

The Great White Throne

Where will you spend eternity? If you are already saved, it will be spent in the presence of God; if you are not saved, I urge you to take this time to ask Jesus to be your Lord and Savior, it is the most important decision that you will ever make.

And I saw the dead, great and small standing before the throne, and books were opened. Another book was opened, which is the book of life. The dead were judged according to what they had done as recorded in the books. The sea gave up the dead that were in it and death and Hades gave up the dead that were in them, and each person was judged according to what he had done. (Revelation 20:12-13)

Everyone that has ever died will be resurrected, that is how man was recreated, with the concept that the mortal body will be raised immortal. This includes those who have never accepted Jesus as their Savior. The immortal body will never perish, though for the unsaved it will die a second death for all eternity. As a human, the mortal body perishes when death occurs and begins the process of reverting back to dust. Death occurs and then it is finished and the human body experiences decomposition, death does not continue to occur in that body when it ceases to function. With the second death, the process of dying never ends, the torment one would feel if burnt alive will continue into infinity or forever, a length of time our finite minds cannot comprehend. We were not created by God to spend eternity dying; we were created to live with God as his family forever. The lake of burning fire was created exclusively for Satan, however, a person's choice to reject God leaves this option open to the unbeliever. Yes, it is an option, a choice; when a person chooses to reject God, then they are opting to spend eternity in a lake of fire, even if they do not think they are choosing Satan. By choosing to reject God, through many avenues such as atheism, false religions, living in sin, moral and spiritual corruptness, or apathy towards God; they have chosen Satan. There are only two viable choices, though Satan would want you to think there are many choices.

Enter through the narrow gate. For wide is the gate and broad is the road that leads to destruction, and many enter through it. But small is the gate and narrow the road that leads to life, and only a few find it. (Matthew 7:13)

The broad or wide road encompasses all the things in this world with the exception of living to please God. That statement does not mean that a Christian cannot have any material things or participate in anything other than the church choir, but in the condition of a persons' heart in regards to the material world. Satan's greatest deception is 'there are many paths to God'. There is only one, Jesus says, *"I am the way, the truth, and the life. No man comes to the Father except through me."* (John 14:6) Everyone on the planet is not worshipping the same God under different names. The other religions of the world are the broad path, Buddhists and Far Eastern Cults, Hindus, Muslims, Wiccans (black and white magic), African and Native American tribal spiritualism and ancestor worship, Ancient Mystery Religions (Roman and Greek), Nature Worship, Cultism (including Mormons and Jehovah Witnesses), etc.

The narrow path is very narrow; there is only one God that sent his only son to die for our sins. When he died for our sins, it bought our freedom from spending eternity in a lake of burning fire. There is also no other manmade deity that has ever made the claim that they would die for the sins of humanity. Christianity is unique to all other religions in that the sacrifice made was by God instead of man. It is a narrow path, because Jesus deserves all the glory, honor and praise as he alone made that sacrifice for us. When a person rejects God, that person is rejecting the ultimate sacrifice Jesus made for them; they will die because of their sin that has no blood covering of Christ that cleanses them of the sins committed. They are then judged and when their name is not found in the Book of Life, they are thrown into the lake of fire for all eternity. If you were trapped in a burning house, and a fireman came to rescue you from the blaze, would you tell him "no thanks"? Probably not, yet that is what occurs when a person rejects Christ and the gospel, they are trapped in a situation that will eventually burn them alive.

Those who chose Jesus in life will spend eternity with him where there is no more death, mourning, crying or pain. The old order of things pass away. "He who overcomes will inherit all this, and I will be his God and he will be my son" (Revelation 21:7).

A new heaven and earth are seen as the old heaven and earth pass away. The Lord states; "*I am making everything new*". Then he said "*Write this down, for these words are trustworthy and true. It is done. I am the Alpha and the Omega, the Beginning and the End.*" (Revelation 21:5-6)

Do not put out the spirit's fire.

Do not treat prophecy with contempt.

Test everything. Hold on to the good.

Avoid every kind of evil.

1 Thessalonians 5:19-22

References

Buzzard, Anthony, ed. Footnotes: "Final Rebellion and Ultimate Solution." Focus on the Kingdom, Vol.13, No. 10, http://scribd.com, Web. April, 2013.

Curtis, David "What is the preterist view on bible prophecy." International Preterist Association (IPA), http://www.preterist.org/whatispreterism.asp, Web. May 2013

Goodman, Amy & Juan González, "Pentagon Reverses Position and Admits U.S. Troops Used White Phosphorus Against Iraqis in Fallujah." http://democracynow.org, 2005. Web. May 2013

Haliczer, Stephen, Ph.D., "The Cathar Heresy." Secret Files of the Inquisition, http://pbs.org, Inquisition Productions, 2007. Web. April, 2013

"TheHolyInquisition."http://www.bibliotecapleyades.net/vatican/vatican_holyinquisition.

Kopping, Wayne "Cultural Jihad in Action." http://theclarionproject.org, 2010. Web. May 2013

Leitenberg, Milton "Deaths in Wars and Conflicts Between 1945 and 2000" Center for International and Security Studies at University of Maryland, 2006. Web. May, 2013

Manhattan, Avro "Vatican Billions." chp 26, Christian Assemblies International, http://www.cai.org/bible-studies/vatican-billions,1986. Web. January, 2012.

Mason, Cyrus "A History of the Holy Catholic Inquisition." H. Perkins, 1835 (not in copyright)Internet Archive: American Libraries, Web. May 2013.

Moderator, "Saudi Arabia: Live Entertainment: Excited and thrilled crowd gather for public execution – to applaud and holler." The Muslim Issue, 2012. Web. May 2013

"Muslim Statistics." Core Article: Islam and Propaganda, http://wikiislam.net/wiki/Muslim_Statistics, Web. April, 2013.

Nasreen, Taslima "She Was Executed For the Crime of Being Raped." No Country for Women, 2012. Web. April 2013

Popham, Peter "US Forces 'Used Chemical Weapons' During Assault on City of Fallujah"2005, Pub. Independent/UK, http://commondreams.org., Web. May 2013

Scofield Study Bible, Oxford New International Version, Printed, 1967, Revised, 1984

"Strong's Concordance #3098-Magog.", http://www.studylight.org, Web. May 2013

"Strong's Concordance #H1463-Gog." http://www.blueletterbible.org, Web. May 2013

" The Third Jihad." Wayne Kopping, Director and Editor, Film, Clarion Productions, Inc., 2012. Web. May 2013

" United Nations General Assembly, A/C.4/67/L.17, Sixty-seventh session." 2012, http://unispal.un.org, Web. May 2013

" Universal Declaration of Human Rights.(5.2)" https://en.wikipedia.org, Web. May 2013

"US used white phosphorus in Iraq." http://news.bbc.co.uk, 2005. Web. May 2013

"White Phosphorus (WP)." http://globalsecurity.org., 2005. Web. May 2013

"10 Worst Popes of All Time." http://www.oddee.com, Web. April 2013

Zakalwe, Cheradenine "UK: Muslim Brotherhood infiltration in the British Government." The Muslim Issue, 2012. Web. April 2013

* 9 7 8 0 6 1 5 8 5 4 6 2 5 *